ONE NATIVE LIFE

RICHARD WAGAMESE

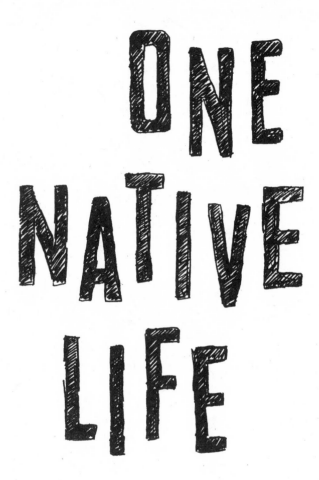

ONE NATIVE LIFE

DOUGLAS & McINTYRE
Vancouver/Toronto/Berkeley

Douglas & McIntyre Ltd.
2323 Quebec Street, Suite 201
Vancouver, British Columbia
Canada v5t 4s7
www.douglas-mcintyre.com

Library and Archives Canada Cataloguing in Publication
Wagamese, Richard
One Native life / Richard Wagamese.

ISBN 978-1-55365-364-6

1. Wagamese, Richard. 2. Ojibwa Indians—Biography.
3. Indian authors—Canada—Biography. 4. Authors, Canadian
(English)—20th century—Biography. I. Title.
E99.c6w338 2008   c813'.54   c2008-902676-4

Editing by Barbara Pulling
Jacket design by Jessica Sullivan & Peter Cocking
Jacket photograph by Tom Schierlitz/Getty Images
Interior design by Peter Cocking
Printed and bound in Canada by Friesens
Printed on acid-free paper that is forest friendly (100% post-
consumer recycled paper) and has been processed chlorine free.
Distributed in the U.S. by Publishers Group West

We gratefully acknowledge the financial support of the Canada
Council for the Arts, the British Columbia Arts Council, the Province
of British Columbia through the Book, Publishing Tax Credit, and
the Government of Canada through the Book Publishing Industry
Development Program (BPIDP) for our publishing activities.

For Debra,
for all the mornings of the world...

. . .

Defenceless under the night
Our world in stupor lies;
Yet, dotted everywhere,
Ironic points of light
Flash out wherever the Just
Exchange their messages:
May I, composed like them
Of Eros and of dust,
Beleaguered by the same
Negation and despair,
Show an affirming flame.

W.H. AUDEN, "SEPTEMBER 1, 1939"

Contents

. . .

Acknowledgements

. . .

MY HEARTFELT THANKS go out to all the producers and editors who saw the worth of these stories and broadcast or printed them. Deb and I are immensely grateful to the *Yukon News*, the *Calgary Herald*, the *Native Journal*, the *Wawatay News*, the *Anishinabek News*, the *First Nations Drum* and *Canadian Dimension*. I am deeply appreciative of the efforts of Missinippi Broadcasting of La Ronge, Saskatchewan; the Native Communications Society of the Northwest Territories; the Wawatay Radio of Sioux Lookout, Ontario; and, especially, of CFJC-TV in Kamloops, British Columbia. Among our southern neighbours, I'd like to thank *News from Indian Country* in Hayward, Wisconsin; *Indian Country Today* in Oneida, New York; and *Native American Times* in Oklahoma for bringing these stories to their communities.

Of course, none of these stories would ever have seen the light of morning without the love, care and guidance of Dr. Charles Brasfield of the North Shore Stress and Anxiety Clinic in North Vancouver, British Columbia, or, in earlier times, of Dr. Lyn MacBeath.

Thanks and a holler over the back fence to the people of
Paul Lake, especially to Merv Williams and Ann Sevin for
the barge, the time on the water and the friendship. Our
lives are richer for the friendship of the Daciuks—Ron,
Carol, Ed, Arlene and Shannon—and of John and Penny
Haggarty, Muriel and Peter Sasakamoose and Rick and
Anna Gilbert.

To our new friends Dian, Richard and Jacob Henderson,
we say *Chi Meegwetch* for the honour of your friendship.

To Barbara Pulling, for a wonderful job of editing
these pieces and creating a manuscript; Scott McIntyre of
Douglas & McIntyre; my agent, John Pearce, and all the
folks at Westwood Creative Artists, my great thanks.

Thanks as well to the Canada Council for helping
financially during the writing of this book.

ONE NATIVE LIFE

Introduction

. . .

THE SUBLIME MOMENTS in life are like the
first push of light against the lip of a mountain. You watch
that pink climb higher, becoming brighter, slipping into
magenta, then orange, and then into the crisp, hard yellow
of morning. As the light changes, you can forget the pink
that drew your eye, and it's on mornings when you see it
again that you recall how it touched you, altered things
for you, gave you cause to celebrate.

This book was born in the hush of mornings.

There's a lake that sits in a cleft of mountains above
Kamloops, British Columbia. Paul Lake is three miles long,
narrow, and the land that slopes down to its northern shore
is filled with fir, pine, aspen, ash and birch and thickets
of wild rose, blackberry and raspberry. It's reserve land
that belongs to the Kamloops Indian Band, and the small
community built up there comprises largely folks grown
tired of city life who want the peace that a life in the
mountains affords.

My partner, Debra Powell, and I came here in August
of 2005. There's a small rancher-style house that overlooks
the lake, and when we saw it we knew we had to make it
our home. We'd both grown up in cities. Deb had lived in

New York and Vancouver, and I had lived in every Canadian city west of Toronto. Both of us were approaching our fifties that late summer, and we'd grown tired of the clamour and clangour of Burnaby, British Columbia, where we'd met and lived together up until then. We sought a haven, and as we walked the half-acre lot the house sat on, we felt as though we'd found it.

It was a house, but right from the beginning we called it our cabin. It had been built by a seventy-two-year-old Swede named Walter Jorgenson, and the place showed the hand and eye of a single septuagenarian. The carpets were mouldy. The cabin hadn't seen a paint job in some time. The deck was unfinished, and the house badly needed a roof. Still, the land it sat upon sang to us, and we found a way to make it ours.

A gravel road curves from the main road to the lakeshore. My dog, Molly, and I began to make a stroll down to the water every morning. The land settled around my shoulders. On those morning walks I breathed in the crisp mountain air and felt it ease me into a peace I had seldom experienced. I felt reconnected to my Ojibway self. The more I presented myself to the land in those early hours, the more it offered me back the realization of who I was created to be.

I began to remember. The sound of squirrels in the topmost branches of a pine tree reminded me of a forgotten episode from my boyhood; the wobbly call of the loons took me back to an adventure on the land when I was a young man. And there was always the light. The shades and degrees of it evoked people and places I hadn't thought about in decades. Every one of those walks allowed me the grace of recollection, and I began to write things down. I started to see my life differently. Up until then I had considered it a struggle, an ongoing fight for identity and a sense of belonging. Those walks with Molly let me see that I had lived a life of alternation between light and dark, and that the contrast itself was the identity I had always sought.

I had lived one native life. Within it were the issues and the struggles of many native people in Canada, but my life was unique. It was mine. It became important for me to reclaim the joy, the hurt and the ordinary to-and-fro of it.

The first reason I wanted to do that was my own healing. I'd suffered abuse and abandonment as a toddler. My terror was magnified in foster homes and in an adopted home where I lived for seven years. For a long while afterwards I tried running away, hiding or drinking excessively to shut out the pain. Gradually, with the help of therapists, I understood that I wasn't crazy. It was the trauma that had caused me to choose hurt over joy, that made me believe my life would always be a bottomless hole of blackness and misery. Walking in the light of those mountain mornings helped me to see where the teachings and the grace and the happiness had been.

The second reason was Canada.

As I got to know our neighbours at Paul Lake, I realized how little they understood me. Our homes are built on leased land. Our landlords are Aboriginal people, even though the ministry of Indian Affairs holds the actual title. Despite that, my new friends knew very little about the realities of life for native people. I started to see that this one native life, my own, reflected the character, the spirit and the soul of native people all across the country. My neighbours had never gotten to hear about that. Our stories, as presented in the media, seem to reflect our lives only when we're dead, dying or complaining. The stories in this book are positive. They embrace healing. They reflect an empowered people, and they deserve to be told.

We're all neighbours: that's the reality. This land has the potential for social greatness. And within this cultural mosaic lies the essential ingredient of freedom—acceptance. That's an Aboriginal principle I've learned. When you know your neighbours, when you can lean over the fence and hear each other's stories, you foster understanding, harmony and community.

Stories are meant to heal. That's what my people say, and it's what I believe. Culling these stories has taken me a long way down the healing path from the trauma I carried. This book is a look back at one native life, at the people, the places and the events that have helped me find my way to peace again, to stand in the sunshine with my beautiful partner, looking out over the lake and the land we love and say—yes.

BOOK ONE

AHKI

(EARTH)

MY PEOPLE SAY that we are of the earth. We come from

her. We emerged from her bosom fully formed and ready

to assume our place as stewards, caretakers, guardians.

Our rich brown skin reminds us that we are her children,

that we belong here, that our home is always at our feet,

wherever we might travel. In the beginning, I had no

access to these teachings. I was rootless. But in the world

of my boyhood, I always found people, places or things

that grounded me, allowed me to feel connected even if

only in very fleeting ways, to the heartbeat of the earth.

She is our salvation. The time we spend in communion

with the earth is the time, my people say, that we are truly

spiritual. It enhances, empowers and frees us. Looking

back, I see that as true.

The Language of Fishermen

. . .

I HAD A HERO when I was six. He wasn't a
hockey player, a rock 'n' roll icon, a comic book hero
or even a movie star. He was a mechanic, a tall, slender,
chain-smoking grease monkey who smelled of oil, tobacco
and Old Spice aftershave.

His name was Joe Tacknyk, and he was a Ukrainian
Canadian. He was a quiet, reflective man who cackled
when he laughed, told stories of Jimmie Rodgers, the Old
Chisholm Trail and life during wartime. He was my foster
father. I came to live with him and his family when I was
five. He saw the fear in me from that first moment, the
confusion, and did what he could to make them disappear.

He'd come for me early spring and summer mornings.
He'd scratch at the soles of my feet with a wooden spoon
and hush me to silence with a finger to the lips. Then,
while everyone else slept, he made an elaborate game of
sneaking me from the house with our fishing gear and into
the old green pickup truck in the driveway.

As we drove out of Kenora, Ontario, on the gravel road
that ran north from town, he'd slip me a cup of coffee and
some warm perogies wrapped in a napkin. We'd watch

the land roll by, and the silence we sat in was as profound as any I've ever experienced. There was nothing to say. Mystery. We sat in the hold of the mystery of the land. There were no words to describe that feeling.

When we got to the marina, my job was to load the gear in the old wooden boat while Joe hooked up the gas tank. Then we'd pull away from the dock and he'd look at me. I'd scan the water of the river, pick a direction and point, and he'd head us that way. Once he'd found a cove or a bay or a rock point somewhere we'd start to cast. Wordlessly. Always. The only language we used was the quiet way of fishermen, the nod, the gesture when we needed tackle, each of us content to look at the land and the water and the deep endless bowl of the sky.

I landed a huge jackfish one morning. When it hit my bait, the rod bowed under the keel of the boat, and I could feel the whale-like pressure of the fish at the other end. Joe sat and watched me. The only words he offered were cautionary ones, cryptic tips on how to play it. After twenty minutes or so he netted the exhausted fish and hoisted it into the boat. It was enormous. My hands were sore from clenching the rod, but I held that fish up by the gill case and felt proud and noble and strong. He smiled at me, ruffled my hair some and went back to casting, but I knew he was proud of me. That made the effort worth it.

We let that fish go. I sat in the boat and watched it heave for breath, and something in me understood that it was the battle that was memorable and the fish deserved to live to fight another day. Something in me understood that I'd been graced with some of the spirit of that magnificent creature and that it could be free again. I asked him and he looked at me quizzically for a moment, then nodded and helped me ease the fish back over the side of the boat.

We never spoke of it after. Never shared that moment with the rest of my foster family. But there was an unspoken bond between us, and I knew that I had earned his respect. I could see it in the way he looked at me when we were on the water, like an equal, like a partner, like a man. I've never forgotten that.

Joe understood that I was Ojibway. He understood that I needed a connection to the land to feel safe, real, right. He also understood that there were things in me I could not express, and he gave me the language of fishermen so I could start to find the words.

Of all the men who came into my life as I was growing up, Joe Tacknyk was the one who fostered "father" in me. He gave the word meaning. See, Joe understood that we all have one basic human right coming in—the right to know who we are created to be. He took the responsibility to show me that in the only way he could.

For me, at six, fishing was as close as I could get to my roots. Joe got me to the land because he knew that was where my spirit could renew and reclaim itself. He knew that who I was, who I was born to be, was directly connected to the land and its mystery. He got me there. Always.

Cancer claimed Joe a year after I was adopted by another family at age nine. When I heard I took a long walk on the land and breathed the news deep into me. The tears that landed on the grass that day were tears of gratitude. He was my hero, Joe Tacknyk, and I would never forget him.

I don't fish now as much as I once did, don't get out on the water as often as I might like, don't surround myself with the mystery of the land nearly as much as I should. But there's never a moment when I don't feel Ojibway, and I can thank Joe Tacknyk for that.

Riding with the Cartwrights

. . .

I'VE DISCOVERED, in my life as a tribal person, that rituals ground you. They don't need to be elaborate in their solemnity or deeply devotional in their application to affect you that way. No matter how slight or insignificant, rituals connect you to the people you share your home and your planet with. They allow you the freedom to breathe.

Walking the dog in the early morning by the lake, washing the dishes right after supper, getting our morning coffee ready the night before, making the lunch my partner will eat at work each day: all of these things root me just like the more traditional rituals of prayer, smudging and sweat lodges.

For part of my childhood Sunday nights were a ritual. It was 1965, and times were a little slower back then.

I was living in my second foster home, with the Tacknyks, and those Sunday evenings were the first thing to give me a sense of family, togetherness and sharing. Everyone gathered in the living room. The lights were turned low. The telephone, if it rang, was never answered. I still recall the excitement as the old Philips TV in the corner sprang to life.

It began with *Supercar*. The heroes were animated puppets riding in Supercar, a machine that could dive under water and fly through the air at jet speed. We watched it every week. Then, as the credits rolled, we arranged the TV trays that dinner would be served on. We did that quickly, because a big show was coming up next.

It was *Walt Disney*. Every week Disney offered up amazing journeys with Spin and Marty, Flubber, Sammy the Way-Out Seal and the usual gang of Mickey, Minnie, Donald and Goofy. It was a charming program. Everyone, regardless of age, could sink themselves into it and disappear for an hour.

Next came the *Ed Sullivan Show*. Once the dishes were cleared for washing up later, we sat and watched the entertainers presented each week. There were still vaudeville performers around then—tap dancers, magicians, ventriloquists and singers. They were show people, raised on the boards and taught to work a crowd, humble and generous in their art. The show was captivating. I saw the Beatles on Ed Sullivan, too, along with Elvis, Liberace, Ethel Merman, Shari Lewis and Lamb Chop, and the great Edgar Bergen.

But it was after that weekly spectacle that the night became truly magical, because at nine o'clock *Bonanza* came on. It was the highlight of the week for everyone. We rode the West with Ben and Hoss, Little Joe and Adam. As we covered the length and breadth of the Ponderosa Ranch each week, we could almost smell those pines, feel the sway of horses beneath us. The Cartwrights gave us adventure and romance and the feeling of family. We never missed it.

We all had our favourite characters. Mine was Little Joe, with his beautiful paint horse. And we all had our favourite episodes, which we talked about and argued over. Mine was a hilarious story called "Hoss and the Leprechauns." Every week we were lifted out of our lives and swept away.

Later, alone in my bed, I would go back over all that I'd seen. I drifted off to sleep filled with images of hope, warmth, community, adventure and the generosity of spirit. I couldn't wait for the replay of that ritual in seven days' time. Those few hours in front of the television made me forget that I was a foster kid, a displaced person, filled with hurts I hadn't found the words for yet.

Television has changed now. The old innocence and humility are missing. There are no Ed Sullivans, no grand production numbers with dancers and orchestra, no chorales or entertainers who learned their chops in small vaudeville theatres, no Red Skeltons, Maurice Chevaliers, Carmen McRaes or Cyd Charisses. There's certainly no one like the Cartwrights.

When you gather with others for the sublime purpose of being together, the strength of that ritual binds you, shapes you, maybe even saves you. I learned that as a foster home kid, and rituals still hold that charm and power. We're tribal people, the whole magnificent lot of us, and we shine brightest when we honour the rituals that join us.

The Kiss

. . .

I FELL IN LOVE when I was seven.

Her name was Wilhemina Draper, and everyone called her Billie. She was the most popular kid in our class. She had brownish-blonde hair cut in a bob and big blue eyes that sparkled when she laughed. She could outrun everyone, and she learned how to skin-the-cat on the monkey bars before any of the boys would even try it. She fished and even baited her own hook. She smiled at me in class one day, and that was all it took.

I was the Indian kid from up the block. I was a foster kid, and that made me different. All the other kids in my class had real parents and real families, and they were part of real neighbourhoods like the families in the books we read in school. They had Dick and Jane and Bobbsey twins kinds of lives. My life was far from that. I existed on the fringes.

Not that my foster family treated me badly. I don't recall a harsh thing being said or done to me in that home. But northern Ontario in the early 1960s was hardly a comfortable place to be Indian. I wore the feeling of being different like clothing. I understood, even then, that familial love transforms you, makes you bigger somehow, elevates you. When I was seven, I craved that raising up.

Billie Draper smiled at me, and I felt like I belonged, like I fit. That smile erased everything. Up until then, school was all about being the only Indian kid, about the teasing and name-calling and schoolboy fights that went with it. With that one smile, the clouds in the heavens parted.

She lived at the bottom of a steep hill. From my house at the top of that hill, I could see her pedal her bike around the neighbourhood below. One day I pedalled my bike down that hill as fast as I could. When the pavement levelled out I slowed down some, and when I reached Billie's house I faked a crash to the sidewalk. She saw me fall. I'd counted on that. When she bent over to check on me, I reached up and pulled her into the wettest, sloppiest kiss ever given. She screamed and ran back into her house. I was left dazed and happy on the sidewalk, staring up at a sky suddenly blue.

The story of that kiss spread like wildfire. Every boy wanted to kiss Billie Draper, and I was the class hero for about a week.

I was adopted out of the neighbourhood a year or so later, and I never saw Billie Draper again. But I never forgot that kiss or the smile that drove me to it. What I needed most back then was someone to tell me that I was okay, that I counted, that I belonged. I was in that foster home because my parents had been sent to residential school and never developed parenting skills. They couldn't offer the nurturing and protection I needed. I was in that foster home because someone had fractured the bonds that tied me to tradition and culture and language and spirituality. I became one of the lost ones, one of the disappeared ones, vanished into the vortex of foster care and adoption.

We talk a lot today about healing the wounds of residential schools. The government is paying out large sums of money to the survivors and setting up programs for them to discuss their pain and anguish. But there are other generations besides the ones that experienced the trauma first-hand. There are people like me, who had to endure a life of separation, of cultural displacement. We need to take care of those people, too.

Somewhere out there, right now, is an Indian kid like I was, wandering around someone else's Bobbsey-twin neighbourhood wondering why he's there and who he is. Somewhere out there is an Indian kid looking for the smile that will make the clouds go away. He's our responsibility, all of us.

In Apache Territory

. . .

I SAW MY first movie in a theatre in 1964. Back
then a movie cost a quarter, and for an extra fifteen cents
you could get popcorn, a handful of jujubes and a pop. In
Kenora, the mill town where I lived, the movie on Saturday afternoon was the only place to be. Every kid in town
wanted to be there.

My foster mother handed me the money wrapped in
Scotch tape, so I wouldn't lose it. It sat in my pocket like a
molten lump. I fingered it all the way downtown, the edges
of that tape already ragged and threatening to unfurl.
There was the smell of sulphur and pulp in the air, and I
knew that something magical was about to occur.

The theatre was pandemonium. Little kids were yelling,
throwing popcorn and wrestling in the aisles while older,
more sophisticated kids were holding hands, nuzzling,
waiting for the curtain to fall and the lights to dim so they
could get deeper into their first romantic entanglement.

I sat watching the jumble of action around me. There
weren't a lot of outings for me as a kid. There wasn't much
extra money for things like movies. So I drank up every
ounce of that experience.

When the curtain fell it silenced everyone. Every kid in that theatre settled down, awed by the power of the descending dark. When the screen lit up in a glorious sheen, I fell head over heels in love.

Back then, afternoon matinees were double bills with a cartoon and a newsreel thrown in. That day I watched *Bugs Bunny* and laughed. I don't recall any of the newsreel, but the first feature was *Hey There, It's Yogi Bear*. Yogi, as the Brown Phantom, swung down from the trees on a rope to steal picnic baskets from the tourists at Jellystone. Cindy Bear got blamed for being the park menace and was shipped off to the zoo. Yogi and Boo Boo had to travel to St. Louis to rescue her, and it all ended happily after a wild dose of adventure.

The second feature, *Apache Territory*, starred a cowboy actor named Rory Calhoun. In it, a wagon train was attacked by Apache Indians. There was heavy drama as night fell and the hardy pioneers were threatened by the evil savages. Everyone in that theatre sat hushed. You could feel the tension. When the denouement came, and the good guys in the white hats won the day and rode off boldly into the sunset, that was something to cheer about.

I was transported by that movie, taken away from my mill-town life and dropped into a world of light and sound and colour so intense I never wanted to leave. It was as if a dream had been thrown up on beams of light. I'd walked into thrilling new territory.

It didn't matter to me then that there were racist over-tones to the movie, that my people were belittled, made cartoons of. It didn't matter to me that there were snick-ers and finger pointing when we kids tumbled out into the light of day. All that mattered to me was how I felt. My imagination was fired up and my insides quivered from the excitement of seeing life splayed out on a fifty-foot screen.

Apache Territory was a standard western, a B movie with B-list actors, writers and directors. It had room only for tried-and-true characterizations, and the story played well to B-movie audiences. I didn't know then how great a portion of the national demographic believed what those movies said.

We have Indian producers and directors today. Native people are depicting their lives as they live them, and even Hollywood, when it takes the risk of presenting a movie about Indians, does that respectfully for the most part now. When our children see their people on the silver screen today, they see a more genuine image.

In 1964 it was all about the dazzle. It was all about the magic of being entranced. They don't have curtains at movie theatres any more. There are few double bills, no fifteen-cent snacks. I miss the old-fashioned thrill of it all, cartoon Indians or not.

The Flag on the Mountain

. . .

SOMEONE HAS PUT a flag up on the mountain. It flaps and waves high above the lake, up where they helicopter-logged a few years back. Getting it up there must have taken gumption, and the scarlet and white, hard against the green, is a statement to that grit. Seeing that flag takes me back, as everything out on the land has a tendency to do.

Victoria Day, 1965. I'd just been adopted and moved from northern Ontario to Bradford, a small town an hour's drive from Toronto. By the time the holiday rolled around, I'd been in my new home about a month. I felt as though I'd been plunked down on Mars. There was nothing left of the world I had known for the first nine years of my life.

Bradford was on the edge of the Holland Marsh. There, the land was flat, treeless, devoted to the reaping of vegetables. The water flowed through irrigation canals all brown and muddy. There was no bush, no pink granite outcroppings, no cliffs overlooking a lake, no open vistas. Life among the Martians felt restrictive and colourless. There was a gaping hole in me that I had once used the land to fill.

In the school where they sent me, I was the only Indian kid. In fact, I was the only brown face. The Martians were pale, with names like McLaughlin, Reid, Carpenter and Wesley. Sitting in the tight, formal rows of Bradford Elementary School, I was weird, exotic and more than a little uncomfortable. In the class photo from that year, I stuck out in the sea of white faces like a fence post in a field of snow. It was lonely, but there was no one to tell.

I didn't know how to move in Bradford. It was a loopy feeling, like in a dream when every placing of your foot is weightless. The edges of my body had become blurred, and I couldn't find a space to hold me. Even the language, the colloquial urban schoolboy rap, was new and hard on my ears.

Then one day the teacher announced the upcoming Queen's birthday, as we called it then. She went on to explain that Bradford would raise the new Canadian flag for the first time on the Friday before the holiday weekend. There would be a band, the mayor would speak, and a special ceremony would mark the raising of the brand-new Canadian symbol, which Prime Minister Pearson had pushed through Parliament several months earlier. The school wanted someone very special to raise the flag, the teacher said. The principal and the mayor had chosen me. She said my people represented the original face of Canada, and they wanted to honour that.

But when the day came, I was nervous. There was going to be a news photographer at the ceremony, and my picture would be in the paper. I was dressed in new clothes, and my shoes were shined. My adopted parents instructed me severely in how to behave. Up in front of that big crowd, I sat in my chair barely able to listen to the speeches. Then someone called my name.

The band struck up the first notes of *O Canada*. My hands grasped the lanyard. As the song began to swell, I hauled on that rope. The flag inched up the pole, then caught in the breeze, fluttered and began to wave. As I watched it gain the sky I did feel honoured. I was filled with a crazy sense of possibility, as if that flag could make anything happen.

Right then, I believed that Canada was a wish, a breath waiting to be exhaled. I believed that the song was a blessing, the flag its standard. I believed, as I had been told by the teacher, that my people were special, that I was special and that the blessings of that song and that flag fell equally on my shoulders. The true north, strong and free.

Since then I have learned that the national anthem can be a dirge at times, a wail, a cry in the night. I have learned that hidden in the thunder of the trumpets and the snap of the drums are common voices hollering to be heard. The flag is a symbol of the separation between red and white. It's hugely ironic because of that.

But I love this country. I love that flag. The majority of native people do. Every land claim, every barricade, every protest is less a harangue for rights and property than it is a beseeching for the promise offered in that flag, represented by it. Equality. A shared vision, a shared responsibility. A wish, a held breath waiting to be exhaled. The flag above the lake flaps in the breeze of this mountain morning, over everything, over everyone.

The Way to Arcturus

.   .   .

WHEN IT GETS DARK, I stand outside our cabin
and lean my head back to look at the stars. Some nights
they seem so close you could swear you were suspended on
a bed of them, all just beyond your fingertips.

I've always been a stargazer. In the North where I spent
the early part of my boyhood, the summer skies were clear.
The northern lights often set the horizon ablaze in crackles
and snaps of colour.

I hadn't heard my people's legends of the Star People
then. The world of foster homes was a white world, and
I lived in the absence of legends. The only stories I had,
school-book tales of dogs and families, never really rang
true for me. A part of me craved the revelation of secrets,
and the sky was deep with mystery. I loved sinking myself
into it. I hadn't read yet about light years or the rate of
expansion of the universe or galactic clouds or even the
Milky Way. Instead, I was transfixed by something that far
exceeded the scope of my one small life. Magic existed in
the holes between the stars. I could feel it.

When I moved south after I was adopted, the sky was
overpowered by the harsh city lights, and the stars seemed

farther away. It was a curious feeling, being lonely for the sky. Of all the things I missed in that new southern world, the sky, the stars and space are what I remember missing most.

There was a field down the street from where I lived in Bradford. It had been the pasture of an old sheep farm before the city encroached and drove the farmer and his family away. The field was marked with orange plastic flags on wooden stakes in preparation for the development to come. But after dark it was wide and open and perfect for looking at stars. I'd sneak out at night and go there to stand under that magnificent canopy. Even though their light was dimmer and there were far fewer than I was used to, the stars eased me some, lightened my burden.

One night a man showed me how to find Arcturus. He was a fellow stargazer, a neighbour who lived down the street. Neither of us knew the other's name, but we'd see each other at the field. Each of us would stand silently in that patch of open and look up. Sometimes he'd lie down on his back and put his hands behind his head, and it wasn't long before I was doing the same. He'd trace the path of satellites across the sky with one finger, and I adopted the same trick.

The night he showed me how to find Arcturus, the sky was as clear as I'd ever seen it there. The man stood a few feet away, his face pointed up at the sky, and asked me if I'd heard of it. When I said I hadn't, he began to talk.

Arcturus is called the Bear Watcher, he said, because it follows the Great Bear constellation around the poles. *Arctis* is Greek for bear, and it's where the word "arctic" comes from. Arcturus is about thirty-seven light years away from us and the fourth brightest star in the sky. He told me all that while looking up and away from me. I felt the awe in his words.

He told me to look at the Big Dipper, find the star at the end of the handle, then hold my hand out in front of my face, bend the three middle fingers in and put my little finger on that star. Where my thumb sat was Arcturus.

When I did it I smiled. For the first time the stars seemed reachable. All through the years of my boyhood, whenever I felt particularly lonely I would hold out my arm, fold my fingers, find Arcturus and feel comforted.

What the nameless man gave me that night was wonder. There were secrets everywhere, and I could reveal them for myself if I had the desire to search. I did. I wondered. Soon I was reading everything I could about the universe. I learned about planets and nebulae, quarks and quasars, red giants, blue dwarfs and black holes, and I encountered Einstein's assertion that "my sense of God is my sense of wonder at the universe." Years later, when I sat in traditional circles and heard the elders and the storytellers talk about the sky and its mysteries, these weren't foreign ideas.

We all need someone to offer us wonder. We all need someone to share the Great Mystery of the universe, to allow us to see into it even a fraction. Then, when we've discovered it for ourselves, we need to offer it to others. That's how the world opens up for us. It's how we learn to see possibility in a universe of change. Finding Arcturus is a simple thing to do. I still do it, and every time it's like that first time. Because, well, how often do you get to say you just discovered a star?

Upside Down and Backwards

. . .

I DO MY WRITING in the dimness of morning. Outside, the world is a shape-shifter. Light eases things back into definition. Their boundaries are called from shadow, beginning to hold again, and the land shrugs itself into wakefulness, purple moving upwards into pearl grey.

It's good to be up and working at this time. I can feel the power of life around me, and as the letters form on the screen, race each other to the sudden halt of punctuation, I understand where the need to write comes from. It comes from this first light breaking over everything, altering things, arranging them, setting things down into patterns again and tucking shadow back into folds behind the trees. It comes from the need for communion, for joining with that Great Mystery, that force, that energy.

I have always wanted to write. There isn't a time I can recall when I didn't carry the desire to frame things, order things upon a page, sort them out, make sense of them. But learning to write was a challenge, an ordeal.

It was a different world in the early 1960s, harder maybe, colder, and the idea of Indians was set like concrete, particularly in the parochial, working-class confines of a northern Ontario sawmill town two hundred miles from nowhere.

The school sat between the railroad tracks and the pipeline in a hollow between hills above the mill. We kids sat with the thick sulphur smell coming through the windows and the spume of the stacks on the horizon above the trees. In the classroom I was ignored, put near the back and never called upon for anything.

They said I was slow, a difficult learner, far too quiet for a kid and lethargic. They said I hadn't much hope for a future, and after they had held me back a year they just let me be. But I wanted to learn. I was hungry for it. I went to school every day eager and excited about the things we were supposed to learn.

But I couldn't see very well. No one had spent enough time with me to discover that. I was slow to pick things up because I couldn't see the board. Even down at the front of the room, where they put me sometimes so they could keep a better eye on me, I could never discern the writing on the blackboard. Everything I learned I learned by listening hard to what the teacher said and memorizing it.

When I was adopted, I was sent to my first big school. There were hundreds of kids enrolled in that school in Bradford, and it seemed as if I walked through waves of them on my way there that first day. Going through those big glass doors was terrifying.

31

The Grade Three teacher wanted to introduce me to the class, so she asked me to write my name on the blackboard for the other kids to read. I went to the board, leaned close to it, squinted and began to write. I heard snickers at the first letter and open laughter when I'd finished.

I'd written my name upside down and backwards. To the rest of my classmates it was strange and hilarious, but it was how I'd learned, and I felt the weight of their laughter like stones. Walking back to my seat that day I felt ashamed, stupid and terribly alone.

But I had a teacher who cared. She walked me down to the nurse's station herself and waited while I got my eyes tested. Astigmatism, the nurse told her. Terrible astigmatism. Then the teacher listened closely as I explained why my writing was wrongly shaped.

I had taught myself to write by squinting back over my shoulder. When we were taught to write in script, I wasn't given any attention, wasn't offered any help in forming the letters. So I watched the kid behind me and I mimicked what I saw. What I saw was upside down and backwards, and that was how I had taught myself to write. I could spell everything correctly, but it was skewed.

I got glasses very shortly after that, and from then on things were different. Once I could see what was written on the board, my ability to learn accelerated and I graduated from Grade Three with straight As. Even in penmanship.

For that teacher I wasn't an Indian. I was a kid in need. So she took the time to show me how to write properly. Every day, before and after school, she and I sat at a desk and worked through the primary writing books. I shaped letters time after time after time, until I gradually unlearned the awkward process I'd taught myself. Unlearning something is a lot harder than learning it. I struggled to break down my method, and at times it seemed I would never get it right. But I persisted with the help and encouragement of that teacher.

I write on a keyboard these days. But there isn't a time when I set pen to paper that I don't remember learning how to write and what it took to get me there. I still shape my Gs and Ds wrong, though. I still write them back to front.

Sometimes life turns us upside down and backwards. It's caring that gets us back on our feet again and pointed in the right direction.

Bringing in the Sheaves

. . .

I LEARNED TO drive when I was ten, on an
old grey Allis-Chalmers tractor. My job was to pull the
wagon while the men of my adopted family forked sheaves
of wheat at threshing time. I had to drive carefully, so
that the men on the top of the load were safe.

Threshing time was big. Hereditary farms like my
adopted grandfather's still flourished in Huron County
back then, and there was a strong sense of community
along the dusty concession roads. Neighbours had been
neighbours for generations, and folks looked out for each
other. Help was always needed for one thing or another
and, in those times, help was always there.

Bringing in the crop was an event. People came from
all along the line to pitch in. It gave the work the feel of
importance, and I was proud to be part of it. The only thing
I could do at my age was drive, and I took to it quickly.
My driving had to be smooth and steady. When I turned
I made sure I did it evenly, conscious of both the load and
the men atop it. When the wagon was full I drove up the
lane to the barn, where the threshing machine waited. I
could hear the men chatting and laughing on the wagon
behind me.

When we stopped for lunch there was a virtual feast laid out for us. The women and girls had worked in the kitchen all the time we were in the fields. There was roast beef and mashed potatoes and four kinds of pie and ice cream for dessert. The talk was lively and quick, with lots of jokes and teasing. I watched it all with a kind of awe.

As a foster kid I had rarely felt like a real part of family things. At celebrations I was ignored for the most part. There was always a sharp sense of difference, of separation, and I learned to see things from the sidelines. Being included felt wonderful to me, and I revelled in it. Those meals felt like a passageway into a whole new world. But what happened after those lunches is what sticks with me most today.

The men gathered on the veranda. They sat in chairs, slumped on the railings or lazed on the stairs. They smoked, drank a beer or two, talked and laughed. It was as if the work had created a different kind of space for them, filled them with a light that you could cup in your hands, relax into the warmth of the sun on your back. I felt manly in that space, allowed entry by virtue of my labour.

I was a boy of ten, working for the first time, and in the loose togetherness of those people I got a sense of what it took to accomplish things. These were farmer folk, and threshing was something they took seriously. It wasn't just work to them. It was purpose, a matter-of-fact need, and they just got down to it.

You could tell the way they felt about the land. It was in their easy talk and the way they squinted earnestly at the fields, maybe rubbed a head of wheat in their palms, then sniffed deeply with their eyes closed. The land defined them, gave them substance, gave them breath.

Years later, working with my people, I'd see that connection again. It was in the easy talk of the elders, the way they squinted earnestly at the land, maybe rubbed a bit of sage or cedar in their hands, then sniffed deeply with their eyes closed. The land defined them, gave them substance, gave them breath.

It takes togetherness to accomplish things. Unity. A common purpose. That's what I learned when I learned to drive.

These days there's a lot of talk about land claims and treaty rights. There's a lot of anxiety about someone losing while someone gains. There's a lot of concern about the land. But we're all neighbours. That's the plain and simple truth of it. Whether we live on concession roads, on paved avenues or along the hard line of the highways that shape the grid of this country, we're neighbours. We've lived together for some time now, generations, and this work requires us to come together.

The trouble is, many confusing things have been said and written. We've become victims of misinformation, and the time for straight talk, for an earnest leaning-over-the-back-fence kind of talk between neighbours, is here. You learn more by looking in the eyes of folks. I learned that in the fields of my boyhood.

Land claims and treaty rights are old promises, made when the country was young. They're not new deals based on greed. They're not acts of revenge or retribution. They're a request from one group of people to another for the honouring of a promise, a pact, a deal made square while standing on the land.

This land defines all of us. It gives us substance. The honouring of a promise is as important to native people as it is to farmer folk. There's no right or wrong in this. There's only honour and dishonour. That's the straight fact of it. There's only the harvesting of a common future, neighbours rallying to get the job done, bringing it home, the drive smooth and measured so as not to topple anyone.

My Nine-Volt Heart

. . .

I WAS GIVEN a radio when I was ten. It was an old General Electric transistor, brown with a vintage 1950s look, about the size of a pencil case. The radio was a reward for doing the chores assigned to me in my adopted home. I'd been there about a year, and that radio was the first thing I recall ever being able to call my own.

I took it everywhere with me. It sat beside me while I trimmed the hedges and weeded the flower beds. When I did my homework it sat within reach in case a favourite song came up, and I even arranged a way to carry it in the handlebar basket of my bicycle. Every week at allowance time I ran to the corner store for one of the nine-volt batteries that kept it going.

I heard the Rolling Stones for the first time on that radio. I heard Curt Gowdy call the 1966 World Series between the Baltimore Orioles and the Los Angeles Dodgers. China developed the H-bomb in 1967, the first heart transplant was performed in South Africa, the United States began bombing Hanoi, Jayne Mansfield was killed in a car crash and Muhammad Ali lost the heavyweight title because he wouldn't fight in Vietnam. I heard all of that on my radio.

It was as if the world had come within my reach. I was a ten-year-old kid in a small Canadian city, and it often didn't feel like there was much going on. Through that radio I came to see life as larger, more brilliant, more complex. But what I remember most were the nights. I would huddle beneath my sheets with a penlight and that old radio, turning the dial and searching out signals from what seemed like an endless universe of sounds, then writing down the frequencies so I would never lose them.

I discovered the blues out of Chicago: B.B. King, Ruth Brown, Big Joe Turner and the raspy, old-time sound of Robert Johnson. Another night I heard Lefty Frizzell, Bob Wills and His Texas Playboys, and the high lonesome sound of traditional country music on a station out of Tennessee. It was the 1960s, so I heard the great developing thunder of rock 'n' roll from Detroit and Cleveland. Deep in the purple midnight of my youth, I heard jazz from Buffalo and Toronto. I learned the sounds of jubilation, melancholy and aching solemnity.

I heard Mahalia Jackson sing gospel late one night as the rain spattered against my window. Another night, when the moon was full and the air didn't seem to move at all, I heard Billie Holiday sing about the strange fruit hanging from trees in the southern U.S. The loneliness and loss in that voice touched something inside me, and I cried. And there is never a time when I hear Frank Sinatra sing "In The Wee Small Hours of the Morning" that I don't return to my cave beneath the sheets.

Everywhere I travelled on the dial of that little radio I encountered something that entered me. There were sounds and ideas, stories and images, people and places that my heart and ears had never before experienced. Because my life was sad then, I allowed the voice of that tiny General Electric radio to fill me. The nine-volt heart that beat in me then was a heart yearning for understanding, for inspiration and for a genuine connection to things.

In my mid-twenties, I found a home for myself on the dial as a disc jockey, a program director, a newscaster, a commentator and an ad writer. Radio was a logical place for me to be, surrounded by the stuff that had shaped my world as a kid. Life called, and I went on to become a writer, publishing books and newspaper columns. Still, that nine-volt heart has never quit beating.

The MP3 CDs I've composed most recently flow from jazz to rock to country to classical. I've heard a lot of music in my nearly fifty-three years. Some of it I cling to, some I reject, but I listen. I learn. I grow. That old radio taught me that there's more to the world than what I can see, and I owe it to myself to seek it out. Learning that has made me a better man, a better person and, in the end, a better Indian.

Wood Ducks

. . .

THERE ARE BIRDS on the lake today. Grebes
and mallards and mergansers float by, intent on their
hunt for the minnows that dart through the crystal shal-
lows. On this rock overlooking the reeds, I experience the
morning as a country, a territory you learn to navigate
by feel.

Red-winged blackbirds, jays and bluish swallows
dart and wheel crazily, snaring insects in the slice of sun
between the mountains. Against the treed rim of the far
shore, loons offer their wobbly cries. In the reeds there's
a thin grey poke of heron, mute and patient. A pair of
Canada geese skims in for a landing behind him.

It's spring now, the turn out of winter slow and lazy,
as if the land is a bear sluggish from sleep. Something in
this ballet of motion kindles a fire in me that first burned
a long, long time ago. A tribal fire, even though at first I
didn't recognize it as that.

I was eleven. I'd moved three times in the two years
I'd been with my adopted family. I'd been in three schools,
lived in three houses, learned to form friendships and then
lost them three separate times. We were settled in a rented

farmhouse on three hundred acres in Bruce County in southwestern Ontario. I ached for permanence.

They'd tried to make me feel secure, but the constant moving had done the opposite. In the little-boy heart of me lived the fear of abandonment. I'd experienced far too many departures in my life, and I craved what I saw in the families of the kids I came to know—a rootedness, a knowledge that things in life remain.

That first fall I discovered the maple bush in the back forty. I went there to watch the colours change, to sit in the high branches of a big old maple and see the gold, scarlet and orange emerge against the punch of blue through the branches. I went back in winter to see the trees' skeletal shadows against the ocean of snow, follow the animal tracks through the drifts around their trunks.

When spring came, the land was soggy with mud. I couldn't explore for the longest time, and I was frustrated. I waited eagerly for the footing to become stable so I could wander. I'd found peace in the bush, and I craved solitude and the feel of the land. Being out there had eased my fears, and it was only there that I felt truly alive and free.

Finally it was dry enough that I could get out. I remember the energy of the land emerging from winter. It was exciting to watch. I saw woodchuck and fox kits, fawns, calves and, in the trees, the nesting activities of birds.

I extended my range to the marsh that reached back from the old dam near the highway, flooding a low-lying section of bush. The water was about a foot and a half deep. With my gumboots on, I could wander anywhere in that bayoulike stillness. Muskrats, water snakes and swimming creatures of all varieties crossed the marsh on their rounds. I learned to wade without disturbing the water, to sneak through the shadows silently, and that's how I discovered the wood ducks.

They were the most beautiful creatures I had ever seen. The male was all green and purple, deep red, yellow, black. The female was a demure grey, with white at her throat and bluish wings. They were sitting on a half-submerged log, and I stopped and stood stock still to watch them. When they swam within feet of me, I marvelled.

The ducks had a nest in the crotch of a rotted tree stump three feet off the water. I climbed a tree about ten yards away and looked down into it. The eggs inside were as beautiful as the parents, tan and cream and quiet. I could almost feel the baby birds breathing in that opaque stillness.

I went back to that tree every day, keeping vigil. I loved the thin *oo-keet, oo-keet* of the female's voice through the trees. Oh, those ducks knew I was there, but I stayed quiet and they came to accept me.

Something happened to me there. Braced in a tree above a flooded bush, peering through shadow and hardly breathing, I came to fully occupy the space I was in for the first time in my life. There was no need for stuff, no need of other people, no need for anything but that nest of eggs, the boggy smell of that place and the feeling that I know today as perfection.

I watched those eight wood duck chicks hatch. They emerged one late afternoon, and I saw all of it. A day or so later I saw them drop the three feet to the water and begin to swim with their parents. When I left them for the last time, I didn't feel the sense of departure I'd learned so well in my life. Instead, I felt joined to them, related, like kin.

The birds on the lake today are busy in their springtime energy. There are nests to build, eggs to lay. Soon, there'll be a brood of young to teach to swim. I'll be here every day to watch it.

Freeing the Pike

. . .

AS A BOY I loved nothing better than a solitary wandering along the serpentine lengths of a river. I'd study the water, searching out the places where fish might be hiding, or lie on the riverbank, lost in thought under an endless blue sky.

Back then a river felt like an opportunity. Within it lay the lunker fish of my dreams or the magic passage away from the world that had me snared. Only in the aloneness the land and rivers represented could I find the freedom to dream and create. Many of my stories were born along a river.

In my adopted home there were no fishermen. Nobody spent time in the outdoors. Camping for that family was a travel trailer parked on a cultured lot with a convenience store a short walk away, laundry facilities and public showers. I could walk for miles through the bush. I could sit for hours in a thicket of trees and watch things. I could feel at ease with nothing but the land. They could never do that.

So I fished alone. What I learned on those solitary jaunts I kept to myself. No one was interested anyway, so they never knew how much I learned of life and nature and the universe on the riverbanks of my youth. More importantly, they never understood how the land, rivers in particular, fleshed out my insides, soothed me, comforted me. They would never know that I was born into the Sturgeon Clan, or that the teachings of that clan membership would define me and give me purpose. Instead, they found me odd and left it at that.

We camped once beside a river outside a southwestern Ontario town called Tara. The family parked their trailer in a small roadside area along a gravel road. There was an iron bridge over the river, and I stood on it reading the water. It was shallow and weedy without much current. I could see cow-pies and horse dung along the rocky shore. It didn't look hopeful except for the clumps of lily pads dotting the surface whenever the river got deep enough.

They laughed when I said I would fish it. But that didn't matter. It was a river. Along the shoreline on the opposite side of the bridge I turned over rocks and logs looking for insects. There weren't many, so I opted for worms.

I cast to different parts of that river. About a mile downstream I reeled in a few small bass. That excited me. Even as a kid I understood that the presence of small predator fish meant the presence of huge predator fish. I moved on, rounding a wide curve where the current carved a trench that looked dark and promising. Submerged timber angled into the depths. I chose a bobber and a long leader that would allow me to drift my bait along the entire length of the trench. It was about three feet deep, just over the top of those fallen trees.

My first casts came up empty. But on the fourth cast I watched an enormous shadow glide out of the darkness and aim for my bait. The fish gulped the hook and swam off almost casually. The weight of it arched my rod, and when it felt that pressure the fish exploded, threatening to tear the rod right out of my hands. I backpedalled to get more secure footing.

That fish gave me the fight of a lifetime. It breached the water four or five times, jumping clear and rattling the bobber in the air. The splash it made when it landed was awesome. When it sounded, as it did a half dozen times, I could feel its weight like a truck pulling away. Reeling it in took forever, and whenever it got close enough to the shore to see me it took off again.

I had to step into the river finally. I couldn't lift the fish over the bank without snapping the line. Standing thigh-deep in the water, lifting a pike far longer than my arm, I felt totally alive. As I removed the hook and rested the fish against my other palm, I knew I'd landed a monster. I shook with excitement.

But something happened to me then that's taken years to fully understand. Seeing that huge fish gulping at the water, straining for life, its power ebbing, its beauty already beginning to fade, I lowered it, let it rest in my hands and then watched it swim away.

I never spoke of it, even though they laughed when I came back empty-handed. I ate supper silently, and when I got to bed that night I thanked that fish for the challenge. They would never have understood. They would never have appreciated the enormity of that encounter or how sitting on the riverbank, after it was over, I could cry and feel incredible joy at the same time.

That river pike was freedom in my hands. When I chose to let it go, I chose life. For the Indian that lived in me, that fish was honour and respect and love. They never would have gotten that, either.

My Friend Shane

. . .

THERE'S A ROMANCE to the feel of cold
floorboards under bare feet, just as there's a romance to
the snap, crackle and flame of the morning fire in the wood
stove. The first tendrils of warmth poking outwards are
a hearkening to a new day.

In winter the morning chill is sharp in the cabin, and
making the fire has come to be special for me. I watch the
flames lick their way upwards, sip at my coffee and marvel
at how life sometimes becomes art. It's a Rockwell painting. The citified man sits before a crackling fire, cradling
a mug of coffee with the hint of a smile at the edges of
his mouth. Behind him, the sun casts a slice of orange
across the top of the mountain. Rustic. Charming. Perfect.

It all reminds me of a friend I had when I was twelve.
His name was Shane Rivers. He was older than me, with
bulging blue eyes and big ears, a sort of pre-Muppets
Fozzie Bear. But he was funny, and he seemed to know
a lot more about the world than I did. He and his family
were poor folk.

We lived in Mildmay, Ontario, by then, an area of
farms handed down through generations, established,

progressive, predictable. The kids I went to school with seemed to lack for nothing. Shane and his folks were renters just like we were. My adopted father was a policeman, though, while Shane's dad had to labour for a living.

Unless you were a farmhand, there wasn't much work around there. Shane showed up at school sometimes without a lunch, and he wore the same clothes for days. He got ignored by kids because he was different and odd and poor. But I liked him, and we became friends. We took turns staying overnight at each other's homes, and I still recall the looks of horror on the faces of our schoolmates when I left the bus with him.

You could tell that things were hard for the Rivers family. Even as a kid I could see that. The cupboards were mostly bare, like the fridge was, and there were curls and tears in the faded linoleum. There wasn't much furniture, and there was no TV. The house was dilapidated and cold and damp. There were none of the shiny things I'd come to take for granted.

But Shane's family gathered around their wood stove for meals, suppers of cabbage soup with dumplings, Wonder Bread and margarine, and the talk they shared was different from the talk around our family table. Mr. and Mrs. Rivers took the time to ask each of their five kids about their day. They asked more questions about what they heard, and the meal passed with everyone being listened to and looked at—even me.

Later, the kids did homework around that fire. Mr. Rivers made a game of sneaking in on tiptoe to add a clump of birch to the blaze while his kids worked. We made hot chocolate in a pot on top of the wood stove. In the morning, when the cold floorboards on my feet woke me up quickly, they gathered around the fire again for porridge. Everyone was sent off to school with hugs and good wishes, even if the lunch sack was small or missing.

I'd look back at that worn old house from the end of the driveway and think it was the warmest place I'd ever been. I felt welcomed there, as if my presence really mattered, as though I was family and had stories that needed hearing. The Rivers family had that fire, and it burned strongly with birch and pine and love.

We take so much for granted when we live a privileged life. We expect good things and good fortune as though they were a right. Even so, there's always something to complain about.

I've been on Indian reserves where you have to chop a hole in the ice for the day's drinking water. I've been to others where one wood stove heats a small frame house where twelve people live. In the cities, I've seen single rooms bare of everything but a cot and a hot plate. I've seen people living in basement rooms with no windows, mould creeping its way down the damp walls. I've seen poor folk of all ilk living lives far removed from anything I would call comfortable.

Shane Rivers and his family taught me that some things are more important than discomfort. I'd have given anything as a kid for half the heart that was shared around their fire. I'd have given anything to be heard, seen and validated every day of my life. Maybe an empty belly can be eased some if you're loved enough. I don't know. I never had to go to bed hungry.

But these days when I light that morning fire I remember Shane Rivers. I recall warmth that chased the damp and chill and brought everything into sharper relief—just like in a Rockwell painting.

Chasing Ricky Lark

. . .

THERE ARE MEMORIES that inhabit you like
light. When you revisit them the world changes by degree,
and you become the one you were when you created them:
younger, nimbler, stronger, more beautiful perhaps. In
the space they illuminate you're graced with the ability
to dream again, to become as naive or hopeful or determined as you were back then. That's the gift of living long
enough. You get to see yourself in all kinds of lights and,
if you're lucky, if you're very, very lucky, you smile a little
wistfully at the people and the places you've been along
the way.

Ricky Lark was the fastest kid I ever met, and for a
time he was my best friend. Rick's mom was single, and
she and Rick and his sister, Rebecca, were in their way as
unusual to the staunch farmer families around us as I was.
The mutual feeling of being outsiders brought us together.

Ricky Lark could flat-out run. I never saw him lose a
race, and on the baseball field he stole every base he tried.
We loved baseball. For us, at twelve, baseball was the only
game in the universe. Ricky and I collected baseball cards,
read baseball books and magazines, and talked on the

phone while watching the *Game of the Week* every Saturday. We worked hard at learning the skills of the game. There were hours and hours of throwing and hitting and sliding. We needed speed to be the best at baseball, and Ricky took it upon himself to give that to me.

He'd come to our house in the country and we'd race. The driveway leading to our rented farmhouse was a couple hundred yards long, and we'd run it until it got too dark to see. The driveway had an upwards cant, and the running was hard, but we raced until we couldn't breathe. Every time, I'd stumble towards the finish line to the shouts of Ricky Lark. "Come on, Rich, it's the bottom of the ninth and we need you home!"

I never beat him. I never even came close. But Ricky never allowed me to quit, never made it easier for me by slowing down or easing up at the end. Instead, he challenged me. In the chasing after him, in the sweat and the grunt and the game of running, I learned to endure and to persist.

My adopted family moved again when I was thirteen. Ricky Lark was the first best friend I ever had. But then we moved, and after a while the telephone calls got further and further apart. Our friendship faded into the hubbub and turmoil of adolescence. I only saw him once more after that. It was winter when I visited, and running was difficult. As I walked away that last time I found myself wishing for summer.

Since then, I've been the only Indian in a lot of situations. I've lived and survived most every facet of the life we call Indian, Ojibway or First Nations. Along the way I've reinvented myself a number of times, trying to snare that elusive quality called identity. For a while I took up the nomadic lifestyle of my ancestors, living in a score of towns and cities, looking for a place I could feel at home. In my travels I saw and felt the hand of racism, and I learned to practise the same politics of exclusion—that curious twist of thinking that says only those who look like me are part of me.

It's a natural enough reaction, I suppose. There's some degree of protection in surrounding yourself with sameness. There's a measure of safety living in a closed community. If you carry a feeling of being lost, it can be slaked some by the proximity to people who look like you. The paradox is that, when no one different gets in, your world lacks colour. The process of exclusion only made me lonelier, bitter sometimes, and wondering what it is that makes us feel different from one another. Or makes us need to be.

For a time when I was twelve, there were no white men and no Indians. There was only baseball. There was only life, and the friendship of a blue-eyed kid who could run like the wind. When I go back there now, there are only the subtle shadings of the love of something beyond ourselves and the joy we found in that together. That's the thing, really. Learning to love something beyond yourself. When you can do that, when you can expand yourself to include something foreign, you find parts of yourself you never knew existed. In that we're all the same.

And the reward is that one day, when my eyes close for the last time, there will be the voice of a blue-eyed kid shouting at me from the finish line. "Come on, Rich, it's the bottom of the ninth and we need you home!"

Taking Flight

. . .

THE SKY THAT TRACES the curve of mountain
today is an impossible blue. Cloudless, it is at once near
enough to touch and as distant as a star. You could fall
into it. That's how it feels. Perhaps there are cosmic particles deep inside us that make us one with sky and space.
I wonder if, as my people say, Star People graced us with
teachings once and part of us recalls that.

When I was thirteen my adopted family moved to
the city of St. Catharines, Ontario. The move there was
fraught with anxiety for me. It would be my fourth move
with them in four years. I never got the chance to settle,
to experience the measure of refuge that comes when you
can wrap a home, a place, a geography around you. Leaving
our farm was a tragedy of acute proportions, and there was
nothing I could say about it.

What saved me was writing. I don't know how many
stories and poems I committed to paper those first months.
It was summer, and school was out. Without a circle of
friends, I was incredibly lonely and sad. But I had writing.

My adopted parents were pragmatic, concrete thinkers.
For them, there were no grey areas. There was no room for
flights of fancy or imagination. Everything was regimen.

Everything was obdurate discipline. For them my poetry was "flowery." Cause for a giggle, a boy penning silly verse. My stories were wild, they said, not worthy of consideration beyond a belly laugh.

They never got that I found freedom in writing. In my wild stories and flowery verse, I could capture the feelings of worthiness and equality I experienced on the land and under the sky. They never got that what was left of the Indian in me had its expression in creativity, or that if I could imagine permanence, I could believe it existed.

When I entered Grade Eight that fall, I was ushered into the world of city teens. The farm kids I'd known had had little use for fashion, pose or attitude. Their world was simple and straightforward. But here life was a jumble of motion, of necessity, of learning the code and adopting it.

So I did what every lonely, scared kid does in order to fit in. I did what everyone else was doing. I hung out on the corner and smoked cigarettes. I talked trash and acted hip. I paid more attention to the acceptance of my peers than to my marks. But the more I worked at fitting in, the greater the trouble that brewed at home.

My life became the walk to school and back. Then it was four hours in my room each night to study. Except that I didn't study. I wrote. I wrote stories and plays and poems about the kind of life I imagined every other kid was having, a life that wasn't restricted to the cloister of a small room. My stories were filled with hopes, dreams, happy endings and skies.

And I never showed them to anybody.

But my teacher that year was a man named Leo Rozema. He was Dutch and still held a smidgen of the accent. He had a big nose and grey hair and all the kids made fun of him. His white shirts leaned to dingy. His ties were out of fashion and he smelled of cigarettes. But there was something about Mr. Rozema that I trusted. Maybe it was because he had to work so hard at being accepted. He had to fight to be himself, too. So I showed him my stories.

One day there was a brown envelope on my desk. When I opened it there was a letter. Mr. Rozema had written out in longhand a poem called "High Flight." It described a pilot's fascination with the sky.

"And, while with silent, lifting mind I've trod / The high untrespassed sanctity of space / Put out my hand, and touched the face of God." That's how the poem went, and Mr. Rozema's letter said my writing reminded him of that. He called me a great writer because I could make him feel things. He praised me and told me to keep going. I did.

I am a writer today because of Leo Rozema. He was the first adult in my adopted life who actually saw me, heard me, got me. From my words he gleaned the ache I carried, and he offered the salve of praise and recognition. He was wise enough to separate the kid from the report card.

We live with pieces of the sky inside us. In our cells is the very stuff of space. The arc of our travel is wonderful to see, the trail of it incandescent, joined to an impossible blue.

A Kindred Spirit

. . .

THERE ARE FOALS on the range land. Against the high-sky heat of midday they are flopped on their sides, tails twitching, soaking up sun on their flanks. It's a reminder, I suppose, of mother heat not so long past. Driving by later, in early evening, I watch them cavort. They race about in bursts of speed that end abruptly, as though they're suddenly puzzled at the glee that drives them to kick up their heels and run. They pause and look outwards at the road with their heads held high and still. There's pride in them, nobility, and a staunch sense of identity that's fractured by yet another crazed dash.

My people were bush people, and they never cultivated a horse culture. But there is something about the animals that has always appealed to me. Horses are called Spirit Dogs in some native cultures, and maybe it's their loyalty and good-heartedness that makes them special to me.

I was thirteen when I learned to ride. My adopted family had left for a summer vacation, and I was dropped off to stay with relatives for three weeks. Uncle Wilf and Aunt Peg had a small farm outside of a southwestern Ontario town called Teeswater. I'd only been there a handful of times, and I felt out of place and alone.

But they had animals. It wasn't a large farm, but there was stock, some chickens, a few dogs and a knot of barn cats. Uncle Wilf assigned me barn chores to do every day. Every morning I gathered eggs from the henhouse. I shovelled stalls in the afternoon and helped hay and feed the cattle in the evening. It never felt like work to me. The presence of the animals was comforting, and even the huge Hereford bull in the back stall didn't faze me.

It was the pony that fascinated me most. She was a small Shetland cross. The first time I saw her she was dirty, with a knotted tail and mane. She started when I approached her, shrank to the back of the stall and eyed me nervously. Still, I felt drawn to her.

Aunt Peg told me that the pony's name was Dimples. They'd bought her from a neighbour for their daughter Kathy to ride, but the neighbour hadn't told them that Dimples had been beaten as a colt and so was unrideable. She was bareback broke and halter broke, but the heavy-handedness of her training had made her distrustful of people. They told me not to go near her, except to let her out into the big pen every now and then.

"She'll bite you," Aunt Peg told me, "and she'll kick."

But there was something about Dimples that drew me. I knew nothing of horses or ponies, but at thirteen I understood the feeling of being displaced and lost and frightened. I saw that in her, and I started to visit her.

At first I just stood by the rail of the stall and talked to her. She didn't move, but after a few days of this she seemed to calm. Then I opened the gate and stood there, talking soft and low and gentle. It took another few days for her to get used to this. Eventually I moved a yard or so closer.

The day I touched her for the first time was magical. She shivered, twitched. I kept my voice low, moved slowly and rubbed her flank. I could feel her anxiety, but the more I stroked her the more she calmed and settled. Within days she let me curry comb her mane and tail, all the while talking soft and low.

Uncle Wilf showed me how to put the halter on. He had to demonstrate on a pillow, because Dimples wouldn't allow anyone but me in her stall. When I came back alone, she let me slip the halter on. I led her into the big pen and walked her around it slowly. Everyone was amazed.

I got on her back the next day. I mounted off the fence rail, easing down onto her. She shivered, shifted her feet nervously, but she stood still and let me find my seat. We didn't move. I sat and rubbed her and talked to her for half an hour and did the same the next day. Then I walked her out into the field.

Riding Dimples was pure joy. We walked around that forty-acre field for a couple of days, and she relaxed. Soon, I got courageous enough to push her up to a trot. And one day, after a week of this, she cantered for me. Coming back one evening she broke into a full gallop. It scared me at first, then filled me with glory.

I rode her every day of that vacation, and Dimples learned to love it as much as I did. Finally, she let Kathy ride her. Watching them from the stoop of the farmhouse, I felt like an adult for the first time in my life.

My adopted family moved away shortly after that, and I never saw Dimples again. But I still think about her whenever I ride. Riding her was a challenge that I met and won. But it was more than that. It was the first time I'd felt kinship with a creature, a joining that went far beyond mere domestication. It was a union of spirits that transcended earthly things such as loneliness, sadness and hurt. I felt like a healer, even though I didn't have the words for that yet.

We heal each other with kindness, gentleness and respect. Animals teach us that.

Running after Werezak

. . .

I BECAME a long-distance cross-country runner when I was fifteen. In a life filled with turmoil, running gave me a sense of freedom. It allowed me to expel the anger, hurt, confusion and doubt I struggled with, and every heaved breath felt like an answer somehow. After a notice went up on the school bulletin board, I turned up for the tryouts. We had to run three miles, and I finished in the top five. I'd never been particularly fast as a sprinter, but long distance seemed to suit me. I'd never been on a school team before, either, and the day I was handed my singlet, shorts and spikes and became a Grantham Gator was a small triumph. My family, a hockey family, didn't understand that running was a sport. But I felt like a winner.

We ran every night after school. Our coach, Mr. Waite, was a competitive runner himself, and the drills we did were hard: running in sand, running up and down the steepest hills in the area, doing half a dozen half-mile wind sprints. Mr. Waite believed in training the body to its peak, then resting a day before each race. Every practice was a test. But I loved the feel of running, and it never seemed like a chore.

There was a local runner named Ken Werezak who ran for our rivals, the Lakeport Lakers. Werezak was a legend. He'd never been beaten; he was big and strong and set a pace that crushed anyone who tried to stick with him. Beating Werezak and the Lakers was all the team could talk about in the locker room.

When I ran I imagined myself running after Werezak, chasing him on a long climb uphill, passing him and coasting on to victory to the cheers of my teammates. Every practice session I imagined running after Werezak and beating him.

I trained hard. I ran faster and longer than anyone else. I ran extra sessions alone in the dark at night and first thing every morning. I ran home from school and I ran in the hallways. I ran and I chanted his name under my breath: Werezak, Werezak, Werezak. I was filled with a burning desire to pass him in a race, to see him at my shoulder struggling to maintain the pace I set.

The day of the first race arrived. A teammate pointed out Werezak, and I lined up beside him. He was taller than me, heavier, blond and intense-looking. I eyed him carefully, gritted my teeth and prepared for the running.

The gun went off, and I stayed right on his shoulder for the first mile. It was a horrendous pace. The next closest runners were a hundred yards behind us. He looked at me, maybe a little surprised to find someone so close, and when he sped up after that first mile I stuck to him. We ran uphill and down, faster than I'd ever run before. The runners who lined the course to watch were excited to see someone actually challenging the champion. Werezak's strength overcame my grit in the end. He just plain outran me. It was as if he had an extra gear, and when he pulled away from me there was nothing I could do but watch his broad back and the heavy, hard pump of his legs. I finished third that day and I never came close to beating Werezak again. Oh, I chased him. I ran with him race after race, stuck on his shoulder like a bug, but he was bigger and stronger and always faster.

But there was a moment sometimes, during those races, when there'd just be him and me out ahead of everyone, our pace matched, shoulder to shoulder, sweating, heaving deep breaths as we ran. He'd give me a little look then. Just a flick of his eyes, a squint and then a firm nod before turning to the running again. That look was everything to me. It meant I was an equal. It meant that my effort qualified me and that I pushed Werezak, made it harder for him, made it a race. Even though I never won, Ken Werezak's glance was my trophy ribbon. I'd shopped all my life for validation like that.

I didn't know then about my people's legacy of distance running, of messengers running in moccasins across the plains or through the forest to bring news of game or to herald a gathering. I didn't know about the spirituality of running, about that detached Zenlike state the elders advised young men to seek, attain and hold. I didn't know about the exhilaration of chasing a herd for days and days and returning with meat for the band.

All I knew about running was that it made me feel alive and powerful. If it didn't erase the heaviness of my life, it at least smoothed the edges. It released me, and running after Werezak was the pinnacle. Lining up for the starter gun already makes you an equal, allows you the opportunity to try. Being first across the line isn't the biggest thing. Letting them know you're in the race is.

BOOK TWO

ISHSKWADAY

(FIRE)

AT THE CENTRE of our being, as at the centre of our

Mother Earth, is fire. It burns within our cells, and because

of that we are entranced by fire, drawn to it relentlessly.

As we gaze into it, something eternal in its flicker and

dance calls to us. In the Ojibway world, great stories and

teachings were shared around a fire. The men and women

we grew up to be were shaped by the tribal fires that

burned in our villages. The embers of them reside within

us today, patiently waiting to be fanned into flame. On

this journey, I have sat by many fires, but it is only now, in

retrospect, that I see how much I learned there, in those

fires burning bright.

Lemon Pie with Muhammad Ali

. . .

IT WAS FEBRUARY 25, 1964, deep winter
in northern Ontario. At that time of year the nights
descended like judgements, dark and deliberate. I shared
a room with my foster brother, Bill Tacknyk, and my bed
was the lower of the two bunks. When bedtime came I
always fell asleep to the sound of his radio playing softly
in the darkness.

That night he was listening to a boxing match. Cassius
Clay was fighting Sonny Liston in a place called Miami.
You could hear the crowd behind the announcer's voice. It
was like a sea, roaring, then murmuring, then crashing
into silence. The announcer was excited, and his words
came out of the darkness like the jabs and combinations of
the fight itself.

Clay was lightning quick as he pounded the lumber-
ing Liston. He opened a cut over Liston's eye and the
announcer yelled that there was blood everywhere. The
crowd noise was enormous. It filled the corners of our dark
room, and when Bill's legs draped over the edge of his
bunk, I sat up too. We were galvanized by the details of
that fight.

I swear I could smell the sweat of it. I could feel the thud of blows landing, and in my mind's eye I could see the younger, faster Clay wheeling around the ring taunting Liston, hitting him at will. I began to cheer for him when Clay was blinded by something and Liston started to win.

Clay recovered, and as I rocked in my bunk, arms wrapped around my knees, I clenched my fists and willed him on. In the end, a battered Liston refused to come out and fight again. The crowd cheered and booed and raged, and Bill and I celebrated the new heavyweight champion of the world. My foster mother had to come in and tell us to get to sleep.

Cassius Clay changed his name about the same time I did. In my new adopted home I got to see some of his fights on television. He was beautiful. He was outrageous. He was a warrior poet, and when he crashed over refusal to fight in Vietnam I hurt for him. In my mind he was a giant.

But my adopted home was a fiasco from day one. No one had told my new family about the history of abuse I came from. No one had told them about the terror I'd faced as a kid and the horrific physical abuse I'd suffered. No one knew then that post-traumatic stress disorder wasn't just a soldier's pain; it could happen to a kid, too.

Physical punishment was the rule in that home, and it was the last thing I needed. When I was strapped and beaten, it only exacerbated the trauma in me. When I was banished to my room, it only embedded the isolation I felt.

I found it difficult to fit in and become the kid they wanted me to be, and there were always clashes.

I ran away a few times and then, when I was fifteen, I emptied my bank account of paper-route money and found my way to Miami Beach. It was February and I wanted to be somewhere warm. More than anything I just wanted to be away.

I got a job in a cafeteria as a busboy and moved in with a pair of old hippies I met. We smoked weed and hung out on the beach, hitting up tourists and swiping drinks from tables. But when I couldn't produce a social security number, the cafeteria let me go. I wandered Miami Beach lost and hurt and hopeless.

One day I went into a lunch counter at Fifth Street and Washington Avenue. They served lemon meringue pie, and I ordered a piece in hopes that a childhood favourite might make me feel better. It was marvellous. When a man came and sat beside me, I bent my head out of shyness. He ordered a piece of pie like mine, and the waitress asked him if he was allowed to have it. He laughed and said he could eat whatever he wanted; he was the Champ, after all. I looked up and saw Muhammad Ali beside me. His training gym was right above that lunch counter, it turned out, and he came in often.

He bought me a piece of pie when he ordered another, along with a chocolate shake. We ate together and he smiled at me and rubbed my head like a brother. When he was leaving, I asked him for an autograph and he signed my napkin. Muhammad Ali. A giant. A warrior poet. I was honoured. Watching him walk away I felt healed, like I could bear up. When the police found me eventually and shipped me back to my adopted home, I held onto the sight of him.

I left for good soon after, and my life became the road. Thirty-seven years later, I still remember the feel of his big hand on my head and the taste of that lemon pie. Finding Ali saved me, gave me the strength to carry on. I guess that's what heroes do—imbue us with the gold dust of their courage. Ali made me a fighter, and I've come out for every round since then.

Up from the Pavement

. . .

MOUNTAIN RAIN is healing. Walking in it in the slate grey of morning you get the sense of what my people say—that rain is the tears of Mother Earth crying down a blessing. There's a freshness to things then, a radiance, a sweeping rush of energy that means Great Spirit when you allow it to touch you. You feel the places you inhabit when you open yourself to them. They cease to become places then, existing in you as a vibration, a tone I've come to call belonging.

I went to the street when I was sixteen. My home life was a shambles, and it hurt too much to be there. So I left one day. I had a Grade Nine education and no sense of who I was. I was filled with anger, resentment and fear. I had no plan except to get out. There weren't many opportunities for a high school dropout with no skills. The street was the only place I could go.

I worked when I could, but for the most part my life became the usual welfare dance of living cheque to cheque, trying to fill the gaping holes in my days. The places I found to live in were low-income rentals, small rooms in dingy buildings, alongside people much the same as me. There wasn't a lot of hope in those dim hallways, just a keen sense of desperation.

Drugs and alcohol eased the hurts, and the loose company that came with them made it all feel less lonely. But the bottle always came up empty, the high always became a bitter low. The fast friends were always off to somewhere else where the supply was better. There is no loyalty in that life. Everyone is living for escape, and leaving is easier since you never truly arrived in the first place.

Sometimes there was no money for a room, and I lived as best I could with the concrete of the city for shelter. I slept in doorways, behind dumpsters, in parks and abandoned buildings and deserted automobiles. I woke cold, shivering hard, wet sometimes, the rain or snow slick on my face. I'd stamp my feet to regain a measure of warmth. And I was never alone. There were hundreds of us. We were Indians—Crees, Ojibways, Micmacs—and we were black—Jamaicans, Africans, West Indians. We were Romanians, Germans, Finns, Australians and Brits. Everyone, it seemed, was susceptible to slipping between the cracks.

You're not lonely for people when you live like that. Neither are you lonely for a physical place. Instead, you're haunted by a feeling, a relentless feeling you're stumped to identify because you haven't experienced it in a long time, if ever. It lives in you like a bruise. The stories you bring to the street are the baggage of a life, and you open that baggage alone, in private moments when there is no one to see your shame, your tears, your desolation. You don't look down when you walk because of the shame. You look down to avoid the shining light of life, of possibility, of belonging in the eyes of the people you pass.

In the netherworld of homelessness and poverty, the commonality is a total lack of colour. There are no pastel tones to your world, only the immutable greys and umbers and purples of longing, hurt, hunger and lack. Colour taunts you always. It lurks on every street corner and in every neighbourhood. Colour. The look of possibility.

You become invisible when you're homeless. You walk the crowded sidewalks, dodging busy passersby, and you understand what it is to exist as a phantom, a shadow, as irrelevant as the discarded newspapers that flap at your feet. Every chink of change you beg for contains the properties that haunt you. Every mission meal served on a plastic tray carries within it the fleeting recollection of another meal in another place, at a table in a room farther away than years. Every shard of laughter on the street pierces you. You find yourself hanging around parks and playgrounds as though you could soak up the innocence of childhood by osmosis.

The feeling that haunted me lived in the lights of the houses I passed on long aimless walks at night. It was the feeling of being expected, of knowing someone was waiting on the other side of a door for the sound of my footsteps. It was the feeling of welcome, of belonging. The feeling of being known. I craved that feeling, and I slowly began to work myself up from the pavement and into a life. Belonging. It's what we're all after. The tendril of emotion that ties us to people and places and things, entwining us in the particulars of that blessing. Walking beside this mountain lake, the rain against my face is healing, like tears. But they're tears of gratitude now.

The Tabletop TV

. . .

THERE'S AN OLD-STYLE TV antenna on the
roof of our cabin. One of these days I need to climb up
there and haul it down. When I was a boy those antennas
were everywhere. In the North you got as accustomed to
snow on your TV screen as you did to snow on the roof.
We have satellite TV now, and though we don't watch it
much the reception is clear when we do. But that antenna
reminds me of something special I learned from an old TV.

After I'd left home at sixteen, I lived in drab rooms in
buildings that begged for a coat of paint and a good clean-
ing. Waking up in those places, it was a struggle to stay
hopeful or positive. But I remember one place fondly.

The place itself wasn't much, just one of those one-
room mansions you can find in the heart of any city. It
came with a dresser, a hot plate, a small refrigerator, a
creaky old bed and a table and chair. Twelve of us shared
a bathroom, and the smell of stale cigarette smoke and
grease from someone's cooking was always in the air.
There was a park across the street where I could sit and
watch the regular folk play with their dogs and children,
but in my room itself there was nothing to occupy me.

Then one day I saw a portable television in a pawnshop window. It was a small red RCA, and I picked it up for ten dollars. The screen was only about ten inches wide, but for me that TV held the promise of distraction and a connection to the regular world.

Once I got home, I extended the TV's long aluminum aerial and twisted it to see what I could bring in. The reception was bad in my room. At first, I often turned the TV off in frustration because the picture was so horrible. There's nothing worse than trying to watch a hockey game when the skaters are double-imaged and the puck is invisible through the dots of heavy snow on the screen. It drove me crazy. After a while, I discovered that if I stayed close to the television my body acted like an extra antenna. I could watch whatever I wanted as long as I stayed within two feet of the screen. But as soon as I moved to get something from the refrigerator, the screen filled with snow and the picture disappeared.

I tried all kinds of things. One of the old-timers across the hall told me to wrap tin foil around the end of the aerial. Someone else said to keep it by the window. I moved that TV all around trying to find a spot where the reception would stay clear. Then one day I set it on the table in the middle of my little room. The picture was perfect. I moved three feet away, and the picture stayed strong. I moved six feet away, nine feet, right over to the door, and the picture was still perfect. And so all the time

I lived there I kept that little TV smack in the middle of my room. It never failed me.

When I think about those days I smile. The times seem so strange, with their outdated technology, and I was a different person. I'm older now than I ever thought I would be, and I live in a regular home. I have not only satellite television but cable, too, along with a computer, a DVD player and an MP3. But that little red RCA taught me something I've never forgotten.

You see, that little television was like anything that connects you to the world. It could be spirituality, it could be culture, it could be a philosophy or the traditions of your people. Whatever gives you your idea of the world and your place in it, whatever anchors you, that's what that little television was like. It doesn't work so hot if you stick it in the corner. You miss the message then; the image is scrambled and the audio crackles. But if you keep that vital thing right smack in the middle of your life, you can move anywhere and you'll always get the signal you desire, bright and strong and true.

Ferris Wheel

. . .

THE CIRCUS CAME to town when I was
seventeen, and I ran away to join it. It was a carnival,
actually, one of those mom-and-pop road shows that
played weekend dates along the secondary highways and
in mall parking lots.

This one was called Wood Family Shows. The owners,
Peter Wood and his wife, Gerta, were carrying on the
tradition of the old-time carnies that Pete had been raised
with in England. Wood Family Shows had a funhouse, a
Ferris wheel, a trailer-mounted roller coaster and half
a dozen game joints. Each May they hit the road with a
handful of other carnie folk.

It was 1973. I was fresh out of work and ready for
anything. Pete took a shine to me right off the bat, and I
was hired to help with the games, the funhouse and the
roller coaster. Life as a carnie seemed to fit the restless
feeling I moved in back then, and the sound of big truck
tires humming down the highway late at night was like a
lullaby. I loved the life and the work, but it was the
Ferris wheel that attracted me most.

In those days the Ferris wheel still had romantic cachet.
A guy could still get his first kiss from his favourite girl
while riding the wheel, and there was something special

about coming over the top of it at night and seeing the lights of the town spread out before you. The wheel was a carnival institution, and I was thrilled to be part of it.

Putting up the wheel was a team effort. Everyone lent a hand. It had to be erected from scratch, and it took hours to level the heavy steel plate that was the ride's foundation, erect the twin towers, haul the axle up and then slide each spoke into place before hammering the pins in with a ball peen. The work was hard, but it was made easier by the shared effort of that tribe of carnies. There was no room for complaining, no time for grumpiness or whining. "Let's get this thing in the air!" they said and bent to the work together.

Paul, the wheelman, had been on the road for more than thirty years. He was one of the last of his kind in the business. He'd seen the carnie life change, had watched as the simple romance of the wheel was lost to the speed and acrobatic flights of the more popular modern rides. Dime days, he called them, referring to the time when rides cost ten cents and the world was a slower, simpler place.

There was no room for daredevilry or risk taking on Paul's crew. Moving heavy lengths of forged steel through the night was dangerous work, and we made each other aware of every move. We used shouts and humour. The teasing and name-calling we engaged in on those set-ups and teardowns eased the tension of the work. And we worked with passion. We built that wheel from the ground up, watching our sweat and toil take shape in the light of the generators, the top getting lost in the darkness. It was pride. Joy. Fulfillment.

I was the spoke puller. My job was to stand on the steel cylinder of the axle and pull each spoke into place with a rope, slide each tip into its slot in the hub and then, holding it in place with one hand, drive in the thick bolts. There was no room for a safety harness, nothing really to hook it to. I stood with nothing to stop me from tumbling thirty feet except a keen sense of balance. It was scary. Anything less than a smoothly delivered spoke would drive you off.

Covered in grease and sweat, I'd stand for a minute after tightening the last of the cables before the seats went on. I'd put my hand out to clench one of the steel cables and feel the thrum of it in my gloved palm. It seemed then as if the wheel was alive, impatient to take on its riders. I'd close my eyes and feel the empty space fill with the smell of sawdust, grease, horse dung and fresh candied apples. It always made me feel good, content. Working on that wheel meant I belonged. But it was more than that. I was in that particular state of happiness that comes with shared grunt and strain.

Getting that wheel in the air was my first experience with tribalism. I was the only Indian on the crew, but working that wheel taught me how sweat transcends politics, how common effort removes differences, how a common purpose brings everyone together. In that, I suppose, we're all Indians.

The Question

. . .

ANOTHER BIG THING happened to me the
year I was seventeen: I hitchhiked across Canada for the
first time. In 1973, the last vestiges of the hippie era still
clung to the land. It was a marvellous time to be young
and free and wandering. There were thousands of us. We
met in youth hostels in places like Nipigon, Gull Lake
and Wawa. There was a feel to Canada then. The country
was on the cusp of a huge and wonderful reawakening, a
reaffirmation of the meaning of its name: Canada, Huron
for "our village."

It was summer when I set off, and the first day I went
from the Niagara Peninsula all the way to Sudbury. Standing there on the great rock spine that is the Canadian
Shield, I looked west to a magical land of mountains and
ocean and opportunity. The whole country lay before me.
The charcoal stretch of highway at my feet was my map,
and I felt as if I could make it to the coast in no time at all.

That didn't happen. The northern Ontario rains
came and left me stranded. I stood for days beside a railroad bridge and slept beneath it every night. Finally, a
truck driver suggested I head to a place called Chapleau

to catch the westbound train. I'd never hopped a freight, but the romance of it swept me up. Outside Chapleau I lurked on the brush, waiting for my chance to fling myself aboard like Woody Guthrie and the great hobo kings of the past.

I made it somehow, managed to claw my way onto a slatted stock car and settled in for the ride west. I wasn't alone. There was a young man in the car named Mick Pocknell, a coal miner's kid from Sydney, Nova Scotia. He'd never met an Indian before, and I'd never met a Maritimer, but we shared smokes and talk and a jug of wine. I learned about the hardships of an intertidal life, about empty nets and empty bellies. I learned about passion for the sea, how the salt against your lips tastes exactly like the blood that flows in the veins. I heard sea shanties sung low and drunkenly in the darkness. For my part, I talked about a life in the bush, about a people who had endured incredible hardship to build a thriving culture and a lush language. I talked about losing all that because of missionary schools and foster care, about how the bush had become strange to me because of it.

We talked a long time, and then we watched the moon rise through the slats of that cattle car. It was big and full and bright, and it threw hard shadows across the empty space. We were struck by its beauty. As the moon rose higher in the sky it seemed to race the train. It chased us into the depths of the night and across the great darkened hulk of the land. We watched it for the longest time, both of us lost in our thoughts and in the magic of that sight.

Then I heard Mick Pocknell's voice through the shadow. "What kind of a God could make that happen?" That's what he asked. I sat in the darkness and pondered it until sleep came and claimed me.

We separated in Thunder Bay. Mick went to a job planting trees and I headed for the highway to continue west. We shook hands, he wished me luck and he was gone. I never saw him again. But I think about him every now and then, and I've always remembered his question.

Oh, I know it was parallax or some rational principle of physics, but on the train that night, the Maritimer's kid and the Indian were neighbours joined by a shared vision, whole and complete and shining. There were no differences, no skewed perceptions, no barriers. We were community, joined by awe and the power of the land.

There will always be cowboys and Indians, just as there will always be blacks and whites, Hispanics and Asians, engineers and labourers, professors and dishwashers. The soul of a nation is in its people, and the spirit of Canada is sublimely diverse. Our differences make us stronger, but what pulls us together, ties us into a shared destiny, is the straining of our human hearts—the secret wish for a common practical magic.

That magic exists. It lives. It sails across the sky once a month, as fat and round and free as a dream. You need to step out on the land to see it properly. You need to walk away from all that binds you to a city, to a desk, to a job, and stand where the wind can get at you. When that moon comes up and begins to sail across the sky, there will come a point, if you watch closely enough, when the earth starts to move, to race that moon, and you can feel our planet spin in the heavens. It doesn't matter who you stand with or where you're from. It happens for everyone. And what kind of a God, I ask, could make that happen?

A Hand on the Lid of the World

. . .

IN THE MORNING, watching the light break
over the lake and the trees and the long, sloping curve of
the mountain behind them, I understand what my people
say—that the land is a feeling. The silence is tactile. You
can feel it on your skin. It becomes, in the end, as comfortable and familiar as an old pair of moccasins.

Life hasn't always been like this. My search for identity,
for meaning, for an Aboriginal definition of myself has
been deafening at times. When I feel the mountains and
the land like I do these days, I remember where it was that
I found peace through all those desperate years.

Libraries have always been my refuge. As a kid I met
Peter Pan there, Curious George, the Bobbsey twins and
the great Red Rider. It was stunning to discover that they'd
let me take those characters home. I loved the smell of
libraries, too, a combination of dust and leather and the
dry rub of paper mixed with paint and wood and people.

The library showed me the mysteries of the world.
There was always something that I'd never heard of or
imagined, and books and stories where I could learn about
it. I read wide-eyed, tracing the tricky words with a finger
until I could sound them out and discern a fragment of

meaning. The library was like an enchanted forest. I explored every inch of the stacks, fascinated by the witches and goblins, fairies and trolls, great wars and inventions I encountered there.

Life changed as it always does. By the time I was seventeen I was on my own, struggling to find work and enough money to feed myself. Times were often hard and empty. But there was always the library. I spent many a cold and rainy afternoon hunched over a book they let me read for free.

Back then some libraries had listening rooms. The library in St. Catharines did. You could take a record album into a small room with a chair and put on head-phones and listen and study the liner notes. I was reading a book about Beethoven, amazed that he could compose symphonies despite his deafness, could put a hand on the lid of the piano and recognize the notes by their vibration. I was curious about his music, so I took a record into the listening room.

It was a dull day in autumn, just leaning towards evening, and the colours and shapes of things were beginning to lose their daylight definition. There was a stillness to the world. I sat in the chair and waited for the sound to emerge from the headphones. When it came, the music was a trio for piano and strings in D major. "Ghost," it was called, and it seemed like the perfect title for that time of day.

There was a burst of activity from the strings, with the piano underneath, and then the gentle waft of a solo violin

before the cello took it away in an elegant note that was
all melancholy, regret and yearning. The mathematics
and the science that held the world together vanished in
the cascade of notes from the keyboard and the wash of the
strings. Something in the creative magic of Ludwig van
Beethoven touched something in me, and things were
never the same again.

After that, there was no stopping me. I first heard Duke
Ellington in that listening room. One foggy Saturday I
played Ella Fitzgerald, the Haydn symphonies, Hank Williams and a great group out of New Orleans called the
Preservation Hall Jazz Band. Once, when my money had
run out, I listened to Big Bill Broonzy sing the blues, and
my troubles became easier to bear.

I went back to the listening room as often as I could.
I challenged myself to find something new, something
different each time. There were always books about the
music I heard, and the books and the music were doorways
into parts of myself I hadn't known existed.

I learned how to live through adversity in the library.
I learned how words and music can empower you, show
you the world in a sharper, cleaner, more forgiving way. I
became a writer because of what I found in libraries, and
I found the song that still reverberates in my chest. I'm
a better man, a better human being and a better Indian
because of the freedom in words and music.

And the quiet that descends on mountain mornings?
It's like old Ludwig's hand on the lid of the world.

A Dream of Language

. . .

I'VE RECENTLY STARTED to run again. It's
more than twenty years since I ran any farther than a trip
around the bases in a slow-pitch rec league. Back then it
was still possible for me to entertain the idea of running a
marathon or competing in distance races. Today, chugging
a couple of short miles, alternating between walking and
running, is darn hard work. The scenery's nice, and the
air along the gravel road by the lake is invigorating. But
I'm in my fifties now and starting over is tough.

Still, there's something big in it, some promise in the
sweat and burning lungs and concrete legs. Maybe it's
the possibility of reconnecting with the youth I was.
Maybe it's the idea of sticking around the planet a little
longer. Whatever it is, it takes me back to a challenge I
faced at eighteen.

As a Grade Ten dropout, the work I was able to find was
less than fulfilling. Part of me craved more. I was afraid to
be left behind without formal schooling, to appear stupid
or unenlightened. One night, sitting in a bar, I overheard
the knot of people next to me discussing a book called
Finnegans Wake. They talked earnestly, and I understood

that the book they referred to was important. They
debated story structure and elements of the writing. I was
impressed by the energy of their discussion as well as
by the idea that a book could drive people to such impas-
sioned heights.

I asked the librarian for it the next day. She gave me
a quizzical look but retrieved the book from the stacks.
It was huge. That was my first impression. There was
nothing on the cover to indicate what kind of story was
inside. Carrying the book across the library to a carrel near
the window, I felt almost studious.

When I opened *Finnegans Wake,* that feeling changed.

The language of James Joyce was dense and quirky. It
alluded to things rather than stating them. The first sen-
tence was mind-boggling, and the first paragraph sent
my mind reeling. I put the book down and stared out the
window. I picked the book up and tried again. The language
was daunting, unyielding. It seemed to ask something of
me that I did not possess.

I walked out of the library discouraged. But the book
would not leave me be. I thought about it all that night,
and I went back the next day determined to read it. I got
through the first page. When I asked the librarian what it
was about, the answer she gave me was as convoluted as
the book itself. I left disheartened.

But the challenge that book represented kept calling
to me. I didn't know why it should be so important, but

I felt the pull of it anyway. So I checked it out and took it home. Each time I opened the book I got a little further. Still, it was a writhing mess of aphorism, allusion, mythology and dream, conjured by a fierce intellect I was at odds to harness.

The book haunted me. It invaded my waking thoughts. It irritated me that I couldn't grasp the narrative thread of it. I was angered to think that a story could elude me. Each time I picked it up I had to force myself to stick with it. Each time I picked it up I was confronted again with the thick hodgepodge of idea and image, and each time I fought my way through. Eventually I bought my own copy. It took me more than five months to read it.

The day I finished it was amazing. I'd allowed that book to take me over, and when I closed it I was shocked to realize that it was autumn. It had been late spring when I started. I understood then why the people I'd overheard were so smitten with *Finnegans Wake*.

It wasn't that it was a rousing story. It wasn't that it was a captivating read. It was because James Joyce had taken language by the neck and shaken it. He'd treated form and structure like pieces of a Lego set to create something odd and fantastic. He'd shown me in the course of six hundred pages what it was possible to do with words.

I read other challenging books after that. I read Homer and Aristotle, Dante, St. Thomas Aquinas, Henrik Ibsen and Shakespeare, all the writers who had influenced James

Joyce in the writing of *Finnegans Wake*. I went on to read Beckett, Borges, Virginia Woolf, Thomas Wolfe, Vladimir Nabokov, e.e. cummings, William Carlos Williams and Jack Kerouac.

Reading *Finnegans Wake* proved to me that I had the intellectual mettle to tackle anything. It allowed me to construct a dream that I too might create worlds upon a page. It took everything I had to finish it, but by the end, I was bigger, hardier, full of grit and eager for the next challenge.

Driving Thunder Road

. . .

THERE'S A POETRY to life that's easy to miss. You get busy, there are bills to pay, changes to navigate, sudden tragedies, the minute details of keeping yourself on the straight and true. But the poetry is there nonetheless. You just have to live some to learn to see it.

My first car was a 1964 Rambler. It was the Typhoon model, with a 232 in-line six motor and the word "Typhoon" in script along the side. When I got the car in 1976 it was not wearing its age well. The original solar yellow was faded, and the black roof was spotty and easing to dull grey.

The car was rusty, and its seats were torn. It smelled a little funny. The exhaust kicked up smoke, one bumper rattled, and that classic engine took forever to get up to highway speed. The Typhoon sat low on its suspension, causing it to resemble those clown cars you see in the circus. Turning corners I sometimes expected the doors to fall off. But it was my first car and I loved it.

I worked at a place called Seneca Steel in St. Catharines, as a labourer on the foundry floor. My job was to push carts filled with metal plates over to the punch press operators for fabrication, then empty the discarded metal into bins. It was hard, heavy work, with a lot of overtime, and I slept in that car a lot of nights. Truth was, it was my first job in quite a while, and I lived in that old Rambler until I could afford a room.

There was an eight-track cassette deck in the car, and I splurged on music. I drove around the streets of town with The Who, Led Zeppelin, the Stones, Muddy Waters and Buddy Guy pouring out the window. I was twenty-one, working in a steel plant for minimum wage, with no roof over my head and no real direction in my life. But I had a car. That made all the difference.

Summer evenings seemed to last forever back then. Friends and I would cruise for hours, as long as I could afford the gas. We'd lean out the windows shouting at girls or drive to Port Dalhousie beach, where there was an antique carousel, and lean against the hood, drink beer, smoke and listen to music. That car was our clubhouse. Every night we went somewhere.

When everyone had tired out and there was only me and the car and the road, I found an exotic, irreplaceable freedom, a mix of asphalt, headlights and music. I drove into the heart of those deep summer nights, cruising secondary highways and back roads with the windows rolled down and the music washing over me.

There was no desperation in my life then, no anxiety, no worry. There was only the road twisting away into the night, and Bruce Springsteen and his classic song "Thunder Road." I'd drive and play it again and again until the early morning, when I'd find a place to pull over, get my blankets from the trunk and fall asleep.

That song seemed to come from where I lived, a land of yearning and loneliness with redemption teasingly out of reach. "Thunder Road" was about cars and girls and the way you sometimes find yourself alone on a charcoal stretch of highway wanting nothing else but to drive and drive and drive.

My job bottomed out about the same time the car did. The exhaust system fell off one day, and the drivetrain started making horrendous noises. I sold the car for parts, for about fifty dollars. I tapped it on the hood one last time to say goodbye.

I hitchhiked some after that, explored the country, found whatever work I could. I was a dishwasher in the Salvation Army hostel in Regina, Saskatchewan, when I finally stopped, living in the basement of a rooming house with just my clothes and a stereo. It would be a few years before I had a car again, but I was never without a copy of "Thunder Road."

There was something in the whine and wail of the harmonica at the start of it that touched me. It was as if a resonant chord lived within me, unresponsive until I heard that sound. It filled my chest, made me want to carry on, made me happy and sad and lonesome all at the same time.

Whether I was driving or not, the song recalled old cars, carousels, buddies and shiny, beautiful girls forever out of reach. The nights busting open, those two lanes that can take you anywhere: that's what Bruce sang. That's what called to me. The idea of hope, of answers, of salvation just beyond the horizon.

Sometimes now, when the night is long and deep and quiet, I'll remember an old Rambler and a kid playing a song called "Thunder Road." Life is filled with poetry. It may not be pretty all the time, but it's there nonetheless. Our job is to find it for ourselves.

Ways of Seeing

. . .

IT WAS 1976, and the dimness of winter in
St. Catharines trapped me. Life was a drab slog of ware-
house work. I was lonely in my small room above an alley,
with yellowed peeling walls and only a radio for company.
Slush permeated me, and everywhere was chill.

As always, I sought respite at the library. One afternoon I happened upon an oversized book of paintings
that had been left in the carrel where I often sat. At first
I shoved it aside to make room for the handful of books
I'd brought to study that day: Rimbaud's poetry, a play by
Eugene O'Neill, essays by Susan Sontag and a biography
of Willie Mays.

But the big book kept drawing my eye. Its cover promised colour and warmth, a contrast to my grim working-
class tiredness. When I finally flipped it open, a door
opened on a new and exciting world. Not just colour,
but hues and tones I had never seen, combinations and
textures that snared me.

The book was about an artist named Gustav Klimt.
He was a rebel, and in the world of the late 1800s he was
criticized for his work. I couldn't see why. Page after

page presented a vision that was startling in its genius.
I was awestruck by his ability to see feeling in common
things, to paint it, leave it there like a message.

After reading for a bit, I came across *The Kiss*. It was
painted around 1907, and Klimt had used gold in it as he
had in a number of his other works at the same time. *The
Kiss* showed a man and a woman wrapped in gold sheath.
There was a two-dimensional quality to it. Klimt had
used the paint to create an ancient feel, Byzantine, hiero-
glyphic almost. It was stunning.

Maybe it was the loneliness I lived in then. Maybe
it was the longing I carried for the warmth of arms or
the desperation born of hanging on from paycheque to
paycheque in a small room in a grey world, but *The Kiss*
captivated me. The passion between the man and the
woman was so powerfully rendered.

The art in the homes where I'd grown up was the
functional domestic art of the late 1960s. If there were
paintings at all, they were amateur oils of landscapes. This
was from a world I had never seen, never imagined, and
I sank luxuriously into the vision on the canvas.

That art book led me to others. I discovered the expres-
sionism of Wassily Kandinsky, the impressionism of Mary
Cassatt, the pointillism of Georges Seurat and the pop
art of Roy Lichtenstein. Each of them taught me to see the
world in a wild, unexpected, triumphant way. I'd passed
by the art galleries of the city but had always been too

embarrassed by my poverty and lack of acumen to venture in. Now I felt confident about visiting. What I entered into was a spectacular world, a dimension parallel to my own. I bought art posters I couldn't afford and transformed the dull walls of my room into a pastiche of jubilation. Winter melted into spring and everything got brighter.

Later, when I encountered the art of my people, I realized those vibrant works had taught me to glean meaning and intent from brush stroke, form and perspective, to find the expression of myself in it, to make it my own. There was no translation necessary then. I'd learned the lingo from the masters.

On the Road

. . .

I REMEMBER THE 1970s as a series of departures. There was nothing for me to hang my life on, no peg, no permanence, so I just kept travelling. If you stayed out there long enough, I figured, you were sure to stick to something, somewhere.

I had a friend who travelled with me some. His name was Joe Delaney. Everyone called him Joey Chips, after a character in a TV commercial. Even though he hated the nickname, Chips was how we came to know him.

When I met him we were both hanging out in St. Catharines, at loose ends and trying as hard as we could to be hip and slick and cool. Mostly we hung out with a crowd of street kids who gathered at night around the old courthouse on James Street, across from the Hub Tavern.

The first time Chips and I took off, we had an old 1963 Buick that threw a rod outside Iron Bridge, east of Sault Ste. Marie. We hitchhiked to a small town called Echo Bay, where a group of locals took exception to our long hair. We had to fight our way out of town. We were aiming for Vancouver that time, but we turned back in Winnipeg.

On our next try we wound up in Thunder Bay, where we hired on with a railroad section gang. We stayed in trailers outside a CNR stop called Shebandowan, halfway between the Lakehead and Atikokan. It was fall when we arrived. and we worked right through that winter, levelling track, sweeping snow off the switches and freezing in the minus thirty-five degree air.

In 1977 I got a job in Regina, working as a manager trainee for the s.s. Kresge company. Chips thumbed his way out to join me, and we rented an apartment. But he was used to a faster life than a prairie town could provide, and he left after a few months. When the Kresge job bottomed out, I called Chips and he came back west, ready to continue our highway jaunt to anywhere.

That didn't happen, though. There was something in me that longed to be rooted. When I found another job, I prepared to stay. Chips hung in for a while, but there were places he needed to see. If he didn't know exactly what they were, they called to him anyway.

The last time I saw him was on a sunny April morning in 1978. We stood at the intersection that led to the Trans-Canada Highway and drank coffee until the talk ran out and he turned to go. He shouldered his pack, gave me a gap-toothed grin and walked away. I remember watching him until he disappeared, the road seeming to fold in on him and carry him away.

My life banked up in a long slow curve after that. But he was my last best friend, Joey Chips Delaney. There's a union that happens when you're disenfranchised. There's a gap in you that only another nomad understands. You don't have to speak of it. It shows in the way you take so easily to the road, to departures sudden, sharp and sad.

Chips and I travelled a lot of hard miles. We stuck together through soup kitchens, flops, fist fights, drunk tanks, hangovers and the back-breaking, mind-numbing work of unskilled men. We shared a lot of lonely highways, each of them leading us somewhere in our hearts and in our dreams. He was my Dean Moriarty. Wherever he is now, I wish him all the grace that those highways finally brought me to.

The Night John Lennon Died

. . .

I DIDN'T HAVE any native heroes when I was
growing up. When they took me from my people and
dropped me into the world of foster homes and adoption,
I was lost in the cascade of mainstream influences. The
baseball players I cheered for, the musicians, poets, novel-
ists, movie stars and artists I embraced as icons were all
non-native. But they shaped my world nonetheless, framed
my intellect and defined my tastes. They helped me to
become the person I am today. Heroes, after all, assume
heroic proportions beyond colour, caste or community.
They are sublime.

In my early twenties I was a record collector. Not
merely someone who bought or sought out the new and
trendy. No, I was one of those rabid LP–buying fools who
waded through the bins in thrift shops and record stores
and scoured garage sales, looking for the great lost album
or classic collector's edition. I read collectors' magazines
and price guides. My shelves bulged with reggae, ska,
jazz, country, blues and rock 'n' roll.

My downtime was spent listening to that music. I made
mix tapes on my cassette deck, and each one was a kaleido-
scope of styles: Otis Redding to Bob Wills, Billie Holiday

to Blondie, Miles Davis to The Doors. Those tapes let me travel musical highways that took me away from my world and its woes. I never thought much about the racial origin of those musicians, only about the feel of the music and its ability to transport me. I was a loner for the most part, and my musical heroes never disappointed me or abandoned me in favour of more ebullient companions.

John Lennon embodied the rock 'n' roll ethos. He was a revolutionary poet with soul. I'd been getting his message since 1970, when I heard "Working Class Hero" for the first time. I hadn't grown up in working-class Britain, but I knew something about being pressed into the shape society wanted and about the pain that drove Lennon's primal screams.

Lennon's album *Double Fantasy* came out in November of 1980, and I was lazing on my couch listening to it on the night of December 8. I drifted as he sang about forsaking the limelight for home and family, about watching the wheels go round and round and basking in his love for his son, his wife, his stage of life. He sounded happy, settled, and I was glad for him.

I used to listen in the dark. There were no distractions that way, and the notes and lyrics could pull you into the heart of the music. That's what I did with *Double Fantasy* that night. John sang about the hard times being over, and in that deep winter darkness I believed him and wished him well.

The next morning I heard that he was gone. Someone
had chosen to remove the revolutionary poet from the
world, shoot him at close range just outside the home he'd
come to fully appreciate, maybe for the first time. I cried
for him. Then I got angry. Then I cried some more. I played
"Imagine" over and over again, then "Working Class Hero,"
"I Don't Want to Be a Soldier" and "Only People," great
Lennon songs all true fans recall. I tried to fill my world
with the spirit that had been taken away so callously.

On the news I saw thousands of people outside the
Dakota, John's New York City apartment building. They
were weeping. They were holding candles in the air, trying vainly to replace the light that had been extinguished.
People of every colour, every persuasion joined in grief
over the loss of an artist who could dismantle barriers
with words and deeds and music. Even in death he brought
us together.

John Lennon always felt like an Indian to me. In
the words and music of this white rock 'n' roller, I found
the essence of the warrior way. That way is not about being
bitter or resentful. It's not about getting what you think
you're due. It's not about blaming history for the condition
of your life. It's not about pursuing revenge for injustice.
It's about living a principled life despite all the seeming crap,
about living with soul, about embracing the flame of your
spirit and letting it burn brightly. It's about embracing the
light of others, too, regardless.

John Lennon wasn't native, but he was a tribal person, and he was a hero of mine. He stood for peace, for understanding, for community, harmony, balance, family, love and respect—Indian values, the Indian way. I wish more people had listened. Imagine if they had. Imagine.

The Kid Who Couldn't Dance

. . .

WHEN WE WERE TWELVE, my friend John
Albert and I were huge Peanuts fans. The cartoons of
Charles Schulz connected with the kid world we lived in,
and we collected every strip from the daily paper. It was
a contest of sorts, really. Everywhere we went we clipped
Peanuts cartoons from discarded newspapers and glued
them into scrapbooks. When we met we'd compare col-
lections. There was often a little jealousy over the classic
strips one or the other of us had managed to find.

We each had our favourite characters. His was
Schroeder, the quiet, piano-playing prodigy, and mine
was Snoopy. Maybe the fact that I have a little white dog
today had its roots in my childhood fascination. I loved
the antics of that whimsical beagle.

Whenever Charlie Brown and the gang were on TV,
I was glued to the set. Snoopy came alive then, and I
couldn't get enough of him. I loved it when he fantasized
about being a World War I flying ace, and even more
when he danced. He seemed to explode in joy. I had a
T-shirt of him dancing that read, "To live is to dance, to
dance is to live."

There was a part of me that wanted more than anything to explode in joy, to wheel about in wild abandon. The image of a small, imaginative dog dancing in exultation of life captivated me.

But I could never dance.

When gracefulness was handed out, I was apparently at the far end of the line. The most I could ever manage was a rudimentary box step, a stutter and clump. I was all elbows and knees, with feet too big for the skinny frame I had back then. It wasn't that I didn't like it. Music had a huge effect on me. But whenever I tried to dance, the elasticity went right out of my body. I zombie-danced. I clomped about looking for rhythm. I could always feel the exuberance in the music but could never express it through my body.

I wanted to swing along with the big bands, foxtrot to the music of a hot jazz combo, watusi with the Beach Boys or even do-si-do with Bob Wills and His Texas Playboys. The dance productions on TV variety shows intrigued me. I wanted to cavort and romp in time with the beat, to throw myself into the music. But whenever I tried I was all elbows and knees, wearing big man's shoes on skinny kid's feet.

School dances were a washout. I seldom left the wall, and when I did I sweated profusely. If I happened to waltz with a girl, I left clammy palmprints on her back. I could never relax and let the music guide me. There was always the paralyzing fear that I would look as clumsy as I felt. I'd faithfully watch *Soul Train* and Dick Clark's *American*

Bandstand, but I could never emulate the moves of the teenagers on those shows. I became content to sit and watch whenever I was at a dance or a club or, when I got the rare chance, to lean my head on a girl's shoulder and shuffle my feet during the slow dances.

When I was in my early twenties, friends took me to my first powwow at the Standing Buffalo reserve in Saskatchewan. There wasn't a big powwow tradition in southern Ontario, so I'd never been exposed to it. To me it was a cultural oddity, something only for Indians who'd grown up on a reserve. As a city-raised kid in a white home, it made me nervous. But this powwow was huge. There were hundreds of dancers and dozens of drums. It was colourful and dynamic, and the throngs of people gathered to watch generated an excitement that I felt in my bones.

The music was elemental and pure. It was driven by praise and soulfulness and a spirit hewn from history and change and a primal love of the earth. It resonated in my rib cage, and the high trill of the singers' voices filled me with a wildness that took me as close to genuine freedom as I've ever been. The drum connected me with something I hadn't known before, and I felt a huge lump in my throat that was equal parts sorrow, gratitude and joy. When I was coaxed out for my first inter-tribal dance, I closed my eyes and felt the drum and began to move my feet. It was magic. I could dance.

It would be a few years before I was graced with the drum teachings of my people, but there was a spiritual connection nonetheless. Once I felt the drum in my chest, the hollowness I'd carried as a displaced Indian kid was gone. In its place was belonging.

It's been almost thirty years now, and the drum still moves me. I still can't do a foxtrot, still look all angles and knees dancing to contemporary music, but I do a proud men's traditional when I get the chance. The kid who couldn't dance found an expression for the joy that lived in him in the music of his people. When you dance for joy, dance for life, dance for the earth, there are no wrong steps. Snoopy, I think, would be proud.

BOOK THREE

NIBI

(WATER)

WE BEGIN OUR lives in the water of our mother's belly. We emerge into the world on the flow of it, and the tears we cry over the course of a lifetime—of joy, of sorrow—are the residue of that nurturing pool. Those tears cleanse us, energize us, heal us. My people teach that our greatest quest is to become like calm water in a pool. Ceremony and spirituality can bring us near to that. So can stories and teachings and other people. As I grew into a man, these tools combined to teach me that, like water, life has ebbs and flows. Within them is the promise of returning to the innocence in which we were born.

Being Buffalo Cloud

. . .

THERE'S A MOUNTAIN to the south and east of us that humps up like a buffalo. From the Paul Lake road, heading west from Pinantan Lake, its bald rock face and the carpet of fir slumped around it make it look exactly like a resting bison.

There is strength in any mountain, but this one is special. Ceremonial, almost. It is stoic, as though it holds itself in, the stories within it spoken in the whisper of the wind off its crest and plummet. Standing in the hushed quiet of morning, it's easy to believe we have a sentinel, a Spirit Helper watching over us.

Such thinking was strange to me for a long time. I was raised in a concrete Protestant reality with no room for imagination, flights of fancy or even the pull of everyday magic like moon shadows or rainbows. There was certainly no place for mystical thinking. Instead, faith sat in our home like a yardstick, a device by whose measure I always fell short. Second Timothy, where it says something about "study to show thyself approved," was big in my adopted home; so was the whole "blood of the Lamb" righteousness ethic. To be a Gilkinson, I always needed to qualify, to prove my worthiness.

I became a Wagamese in 1978. That was the year I reconnected with my native family. The name seemed easier to bear, loose and rolling like the Ojibway language I heard around me. There was no Rock of Ages that guided the expression of it, only the spirit of the Canadian Shield that ran like a spine beneath our traditional territory.

I heard stories of a life on the land from my family. I heard recollections of certain rapids and backcountry lakes, of animals, hunts, paddles to far-off fishing spots and seasons of incredible hardship or plenty. Infusing them all was a sense of wonder, the acceptance of magic as a property of living. Because of that, the stories had a palpable air of humility and gratitude.

My reconnection led me to other things. I found ceremony and ritual, and through them I started to see myself as part of the great creative wheel of spiritual energy that I learned exists all around us. Being a Wagamese was all about belonging, fitting. The name was a relief and a haven, a symbol of my ongoing worthiness.

But there was more.

My people have a grand tradition of naming. A person can carry many names through the course of a lifetime, and each time a name is bestowed is an honour time. Elders grant them, as the carriers of our traditional and spiritual knowledge. You come to them in humility, with an offering of tobacco, cloth and a personal gift. They pray and meditate for four days, then offer you the name that comes to them from the Spirit World.

The man I went to see sat with me many times over the course of a month. We talked about my being taken away as a child, about returning and about the feeling I had always carried of the presence of magic in life. When I made my offering and asked for a name, he accepted the duty.

He called me *Mushkotay Beezheekee Anakwat*. It means "Buffalo Cloud." It's a storyteller's name, he said, and he told me that my role in this reality was to be just that: a teller of stories, a communicator, a keeper of the great oral tradition of my people.

I became what he instructed. I sought out stories and storytellers. I sat with them and asked questions and learned about the role of storytellers in our tradition and about the principles that guide that role. I learned about the importance of perpetuating the tradition of story-telling into a new time with powerful new tools. Then I began to write.

Through the years, I've been a newspaper columnist, a radio and television news writer, a documentary writer and producer, a writer of memoirs and a novelist. I've brought the story of my people forward, and I'm proud and humbled by the opportunity. I've come to realize how much resides in the names we carry. There's history there, philosophy, tradition, the ability to rediscover ourselves in tough times and to celebrate ourselves on days of joy.

I am not a Gilkinson. I was never meant to be. I was created to be a male, Ojibway human being. That's what

Creator intended. The expression of my being lives within the context of Creator's plan, and I feel valid, real, honourable.

I stand in the grandeur of this country and say my name to the cosmos, as I have been taught to do. *Mush-kotay Beezheekee Anakwat*. Buffalo Cloud. I reintroduce myself to the universe in the traditional way of the Ojibway, and this small ceremony is a joining to everything. I've come to believe that, just as I believe that our prayers are always heard, accepted into the healing energy that flows through all of us. *Gitchi Manitou*. Great Spirit. Great.

Making Bannock

. . .

IN THE OJIBWAY world there are two ways
of doing things. One is the slow, methodical Ojibway
method, and the other is the slow, non-methodical
Ojibway method. It all boils down to the amount of
anxiety you want to build into the process.

I learned this elemental science soon after I reconnected with my native family. I had been gone for more
than twenty years. When I emerged from the vortex of
foster care and adoption I was citified, broken down some
by the subtle racism of Canada and unprepared for life
as an Ojibway man. But Ojibway science reached out to
save me.

Oh, there are people about who will say that our
ways are not scientific, that they never have been. There
are those who will say that if the Ojibway had any sort of
technological or innovative sense, we'd have been further
along the developmental trail at the time of contact.
These are the descendents of the people who turned to
us for survival's sake when the North American winter
descended. Science and innovation apparently have slip-
pery definitions.

But the science of the earth is a different creature from the science of numbers and theorems. It's a discipline of coexistence. It's the knowledge and acceptance of the mystery that surrounds us—and the awareness that allowing it to remain a mystery, celebrating it rather than trying to unravel it, engenders humility and a keen sense of the spiritual.

My mother is the best bannock baker going. When her bread comes out of the oven every Indian in the bush comes running. Her bannock rises elegantly. It is spongy and soft and tastes golden, like the colour of the crust. With jam or a thick smear of lard, washed down with strong black tea, there's nothing like it in the world.

She gave me some on my first visit home. To me it tasted of reconnection, warm and welcoming and oddly familiar. It still does, actually. I wanted to learn to bake it just like she did. She laughed when I told her. To my mother's way of thinking, the thinking of a bush-raised woman, men didn't bake. But I was insistent, and she undertook to teach me.

I'd been raised with the Western science that calls for precise measurements and a decisive experimental process. I clung to the security of numbers. But what my mother taught me that day had nothing to do with grams or ounces, teaspoons or cups. Instead, she told me to take a couple handfuls of flour, a splat of lard, a splotch of baking powder and a nip of salt. Then to swash it with milk or water, pat it about until it felt warm and soft, and bake it until it looked good. Once it was out of the oven you gave it an earnest slap to settle it and left it on the counter to cool. The splotch, splat, nip and slap process was odd— but it worked.

That first bannock was glorious. I watched it rise like a little kid would, with my face pressed to the glass. When it cooled enough to cut I sheared off enough for the two of us. It was the first Indian thing I'd ever done. It was the first time in my life I could remember receiving Indian teaching, and it was the first time I had physically expressed myself as an Indian person. It was unforgettable.

When I tasted it I smiled. My mother was a good teacher, and the texture of that first Indian bread was sublime. With marmalade and butter melted into it, my bannock was a rip-roaring success. We shared it with my stepfather and uncles, who were waiting patiently in the living room. Watching the men of my lost family enjoy a tribal thing that I had created was as poignant a moment as I've ever had.

I still bake my bannock the same way. Friends marvel at my non-methodical manner at the stove. I laugh and tell them it's native science, and it is.

When I bake bannock I feel Ojibway. The process evokes images of bush life, an open fire, a lump of dough on a stick and a circle of people gathered in community to share fresh bread. Knowing that I hold an Ojibway skill, a part of our science, instills pride in me. And when the plate is passed around to the usual lip-smacking, finger-licking compliments from non-native friends, I smile to think that our Indian science is being shared.

Sure, it's an easy thing, something a child could do, but passing it forward is what matters. Our cultural survival depends on it. There will always be someone seeking to recognize themselves in the sure small ways we do things. You don't need to be a rocket scientist to figure that out.

The Birth and Death of Super Injun

. . .

I GOT MY first writing job in 1979, as a reporter
for a now defunct newsmagazine called *New Breed* based in
Regina, Saskatchewan.

I lied to get that job. I was almost twenty-four by then,
and directionless. When I saw the job advertised on the
board at the Native Employment Centre, I wanted it right
away. I loved words and stories, and I carried a dream of
writing, though I did not bear the knowledge of how to
make that happen. This job could mark my entry.

It also meant working with my people. I wasn't Metis
or non-status, but being Aboriginal seemed enough at the
time. So I lied. I told the editor, John Cuthand, that I had
graduated from a two-year journalism program in Ontario
and I was on the road searching for a place to settle. That
was on a Wednesday. He was busy, so he told me to return
on Monday to do a couple of rewrites for him.

I was ecstatic but scared. So I did what I always did
when life confounded me—I went to the library. I asked
the librarian for all the books she had on journalism and
reporting. For five days, I sat there reading and doing
writing exercises. I learned about journalistic style and

ethics and what editors looked for in news copy. From opening to closing I sat in the library writing and rewriting. I stoked the fire of my desire with every scribbled page.

When Monday came I appeared on time and was ushered into the back with a handful of newspaper stories from mainstream papers. John sat me at a typewriter and asked me to milk them down to a few hundred words apiece. I'd failed typing in high school, so I sat and pecked out one letter at a time. It took me an hour, but I finished the assignment.

John hired me on the strength of my writing.

That job introduced me to the volatile world of native politics in the late 1970s. The constitutional reform that would entrench our rights was still three years off, and governments regarded us as problems rather than as citizens. There was a lot of unnecessary wrangling over the delivery details of rights and programs most Canadians took for granted.

As a reporter I saw dire poverty up close and personal. I saw people who'd been damaged by the forward thrust of history fighting to maintain an identity in the thick flow of change around them. I saw young people desperate for a cultural linchpin and elders, stately and graceful, reduced to being old and ignored. I saw how cruelly a nation could forget one of its founding peoples.

The stories I wrote for *New Breed* awakened me politically. This was my first hands-on introduction to the lives of my people. I felt the flames of identity being fanned to life within me. Not only was I becoming a writer, I was becoming an Indian. But politics does not nurture identity, because rhetoric is not teaching. I absorbed all the things I saw and heard around me, and because I craved so much to present myself as a native person I became strident and irritatingly vocal.

I was a quick study, and I learned well. The questions I asked as a reporter grew sharper, more pointed and challenging, especially to native politicians. One day at a press conference I was pursuing an issue, pointing and gesturing, moralizing and editorializing. One of the leaders I was going after shook his head and said, "It's like being attacked by Super Injun."

Everyone laughed, and I was horribly embarrassed. But there was a man there that day named John Rock Thunder. He was an elder and a teacher, and when he approached me later he did it so skillfully that I was surprised to find myself alone with him in a small area off to the side of the conference room.

I had it all wrong, he said. He pointed to my beaded vest, moccasins, long hair and turquoise rings. Then he pointed to my heart.

"You want to be the ultimate Indian," he said. "But you have to start from the inside."

He went on to tell me that I had been created in a specific order. I was created to be first a human being, then a male, then an Ojibway Indian. I needed to learn how to be a good human being. In the process of that, I would learn how to be a good man. And through that process, I would discover I had been graced all along with being a good Indian.

It can't work any other way, he said. By trying to be the ultimate Indian, I was missing the most important part of the journey, the human part. Slow down, he said. Be gentle with yourself.

I gave up trying to be Super Injun that day. I began to seek out ceremonies and teachings that would nurture my humanity. I struggled with drink and the effects of the deeply buried hurts of my childhood, and even though that sometimes took me from the path, I never forgot what John Rock Thunder said.

I'm still learning to be a good Indian. But that's because I'm still learning to be a good human being and a good man. Politics could never teach me that.

The Country between Us

. . .

THERE ARE TIMES when something as simple
as the rain that freckles slate grey water can take me back
to it—that feeling I remember from my boyhood when the
ragged line of trees against the sky filled me with a loneliness that had nothing to do with loss. The land sometimes
carries an emptiness you feel in you like the breeze.

It's not a sad feeling. Rather it's a song I learned by
rote in the tramp of my young feet through the rough and
tangle of the bush that shaped me. I come to the land the
same way still, expectant, awake to the promise of territories beyond the horizon, undiscovered and wild. All
those years in cities never took away that feeling of tremendous awe.

When I rejoined my native family after twenty years,
it was the land that framed our reconnection. It was a balm
for the awkwardness of strangers who bore the same blood
and history and wounds.

It wasn't easy coming back. I had little of the Ojibway
left on me and they had no experience with the urban
world I knew. But all of us felt a kinship with the territory
we called our home, and it was there, among the muskeg,

rock and spruce of the northern land, that my family found a way to scrabble past our differences.

We went camping the second summer I was home. We drove to Silver Lake on the gravel road that leads to Grassy Narrows and found a place above a wide sweep of beach. There were five of us: my uncle Archie, my mother, my stepfather, my brother Charles and me.

I watched as they erected their canvas tent, cut saplings with an axe for the frame, bound the frame with long strips of bark and lined the floor with cedar boughs. When I put up the small orange hump of nylon that was my pack tent, they laughed.

As we stood on the beach, my uncle told us stories about the lake and the land across the bay from where we stood. He told us about the portages the people used according to the season, moose or deer or fish drawing them at different times. He'd learned those routes as a boy, he said, and he could find his way from there to Whitedog, a hundred miles away.

My brother and I took off in the canoe to find the first portage for ourselves. It was a calm, perfect afternoon and the paddling was easy. We talked some, but mostly we concentrated on looking for the landmarks my uncle had described. We found the portage without a problem. We hauled our canoe up and over the half-mile distance to a long narrow lake edged with wild rice. At the far end we found the stone marker for the next portage. This one was shorter and steeper. The lake we came onto was an almost perfect bowl, encircled by walls of pink granite where eagles nested. We paddled slowly around that lake, neither of us inclined to talk.

There were no vapour trails above us, no drone of airplanes. We were back in the bush five miles or more, and there were no outboard motors to be heard. There was only the land, the symphony of it, the orchestral manoeuvres of wind and rock and sky. I could feel the presence of my people, the staunch heart of them beating here for millennia, and I felt joined to them.

We paddled back as evening fell. Both of us were touched by the opportunity to experience history, and we talked about how it must have felt in pre-settlement times to make this same paddle back to a camp set up above the beach. We could smell woodsmoke as we approached, and we saw the fire burning in the middle of our camp.

It was an idyllic scene, the Ojibway world unchanged, unaffected. But when we beached the canoe and walked to the camp, we found the others in lawn chairs, watching a ball game on a battery-operated television.

I laugh about it now, that collision of cultures, but back then it confused me. I was so desperate to reconnect, so needy for definition that the cultural anachronism was jarring. I wanted my people to be as tribal as I dreamed them. But time and circumstances had made that impossible.

All Canadians have felt time disrupt them. Everyone has seen the culture they sprang from altered and rearranged into a curious mélange of old and new. So the country between us is not strange. We all carry a yearning for simpler, truer times. We all crave a reaffirmation of our place here, to hear the voices of our people singing on the land.

Learning Ojibway

. . .

I WAS TWENTY-FOUR when the first Ojibway
word rolled off my tongue. It felt round and rolling, not
like the spiky sound of English with all its hard-edged
consonants. When I spoke that word aloud, I felt as if I'd
truly spoken for the first time in my life.

That first word opened the door to my culture. When
I spoke it I stepped over the threshold into a new way of
understanding myself and my place in the world. Until
then I had been like a guest in my own life, standing
around waiting for someone to explain things for me.
That one word made me an inhabitant.

It was *peendigaen.* Come in. *Peendigaen,* spoken with
an outstretched hand and a rolling of the wrist. A beckon-
ing. Come in. Welcome. This is where you belong. I had
never encountered an English word with such resonance.

I felt awkward speaking Ojibway at first. There's a
softness to the language that's off-putting when you first
begin. It's almost as if timelessness had a vocabulary.
But with each enunciation that one word gained strength,
clarity. I had the sensation I was speaking a language that

had existed for longer than any the world had ever known. The feeling of Ojibway in my throat was permanence. I stood on unknown territory whose sweep was compelling. *Peendigaen.* Come in. With that one word, I walked fully into the world of my people.

I learned more words after that. Then I struggled to put whole sentences together. I made a lot of mistakes. I was used to English structure, and I created sentences that were awkward and wrong. People laughed when they heard me, and I understood cultural embarrassment. It made me feel like quitting, as if staying with English could spare me the laughter of my people.

Then I heard a wise woman talk at a conference. She spoke of being removed from her culture, unplugged from it and set aside like an old toaster. But she remained a toaster, she said, and the day came when someone plugged her back in and the electricity flowed. She became functional again, and the tool of her reawakening was her language.

She spoke of the struggle to relearn her talk. She spoke of the same embarrassment I felt, of being an oddity among her own. She spoke about the difficulty in getting past the cultural shame and reaching out for her talk with every fibre of her being. And she spoke of the warm wash of the language on the hurts she'd carried all her life, how the soft roll of the talk was like a balm for her spirit. Then she spoke of prayer.

Praying in her language was like having the ear of Creator for the first time. She felt heard and blessed and healed. It hadn't been much, she said. Just a few words of gratitude, like prayers should be, but the words had gone outwards from her and become a part of the whole, a portion of the great sacred breath of Creation. She understood then, she said, that our talk is sacred, and speaking it is the way we reconnect to our own sacredness.

We owe it to others to pass our language on. That was the other thing she said. If we have even one word of our talk, then we have a responsibility to pass it on to our children and to those who have had the language removed from them. We learn to speak for them. We learn to speak so we can serve as a tool for someone else's reconnection.

I'm still far from fluent. I still spend far more time using English, but the Ojibway talk sits there in the middle of my chest like a hope. When I use it—in a prayer, in a greeting, in a talk somewhere—I feel the same sensation I did with that first word at age twenty-four—the feeling of being ushered in, of welcome, of familiarity and belonging.

An English word I admire is "reclaim." It means "to bring back, to return to a proper course." When I learned to speak Ojibway I reclaimed a huge part of myself. It wasn't lost, I had always owned it; it was just adrift on the great sea of influence that is the modern world. Like a mariner lost upon foreign seas, I sought a friendly shore to step out on so I could learn to walk again. My language became that shore.

I introduce myself by my Ojibway name, according to our traditional protocols, whenever I give a talk. I can ask important questions in my language. I can greet people in the proper manner, and I can pray.

For me, *peendigaen*, come in, meant I could express myself as who I was created to be. That's what this journey is all about—to learn to express yourself as whom you were created to be. You don't need to be a native person to understand that.

The Animal People

. . .

LAST WEEK WE SAW wolves on the ice. There
were two of them, a large dark male and a smaller, dusky-
coloured female. It's the beginning of winter, and the ice
has just set on the lake a few miles down the road from
our cabin. I spotted them out of the corner of my eye,
two dark dots on a sheet of white.

They lingered a few days. It was the sun, I think. The
last vestiges of autumn sun warmed the flat pan of the
lake, and the wolves lay there soaking it in, before the cold
fingers of winter pushed it from the sky. Transients, headed
through this territory on their way north into the backcountry for winter.

There's a lot of animal life in the area. Black bears,
bobcats, muskrats, beavers, even the odd rumour of
cougars sliding out of view through the pine trees. But
seeing the wolves made me smile. There's a primeval connection to *Myeengun*, as the wolf is called in Ojibway.
It pulls at my consciousness, even though I don't fully
understand it.

I've always been an animal guy. I never had a pet when
I was small, but I was always drawn to the dogs and cats

in my neighbourhood. I was a Young Naturalist for a while; that was a mail-in club for youngsters eager to learn outdoor skills. When I was a kid, it was the closest I could get to native teachings.

Back then, I didn't have the benefit of the animal stories told by our traditional storytellers. I didn't know that Ojibway people regard animals as their greatest teachers. I never knew as a kid that Ojibway people referred to four-legged creatures as Animal People. It wouldn't have struck me as odd, though. I think I've always regarded them in that way.

Soon after reconnecting with my tribal family, I was walking with my uncle on the traditional land we'd once trapped on. It had snowed the night before, and a couple of inches lay on the ground. Sound was softened, and we moved like ghosts. Everywhere the detail of things was cut into sharp relief by the blanket of white. It was as if the land was magnified somehow, heightened. Seeing it that way was like seeing it for the first time. I was enthralled.

There was a sudden set of tracks in the snow. They cut across our path and disappeared into the thick bush, like a thought. As I stood studying them, my uncle looked around us casually and asked no one in particular, "I wonder who passed here?"

It seemed a strange question. He made it sound as if the tracks belonged to a person. His reaction puzzled me, so I asked him about it.

He told me that when Creator sent Human Beings to live in this reality, he called the Animals forward and directed them to remain our teachers forever. Their teachings showed the Human Beings how to relate to the world and how to treat the earth. What the Ojibway know of ourselves as people, such as our need to live in harmony with each other, came to us from the Animal People.

As we walked, my uncle told me legends and traditional stories: how the dog came to be man's greatest friend, why the wolverine is a loner and why the raven is black. Each story was like a world, and entering them I felt bigger, sketched out more fully. I could see why my uncle said "who" instead of "what" when we passed those tracks in the snow.

We are all related. That's what my people understood from the earliest times. At the core of each of us is the creative energy of the universe. Every being and every form shares that kinetic, world-building energy. It makes us brothers, sisters, kin, family. Ojibway teachings tell us that we all come out of the earth, that we belong here, that we share this planet equally, animals and people. Walking with my uncle that winter day, I came to the beginning of understanding that.

Finding the Old Ones

. . .

THERE ARE SILENCES that reside in you like a dream undreamed. I have found them at the edges of great precipices in the Rockies and on the glassine surface of northern lakes, watching the bottom over the bow of the canoe, the movement like flying. The quiet that descends at the end of a good talk can tell you more than all the spoken words. It's a big old noisy world, and a remembered silence takes you away from that clatter, returns you to a moment when all you knew of life was where you stood—and it was enough.

My life was full of noise for a long, long time. The internal clamour of a scared, lonely foster kid rang through everything I tried, everywhere I went. But when I was twenty-four I found silence.

By then I'd spent a hard eight years searching for a place to fit. I'd been across the country a few times, worked at various things, quit and moved on, prowling Canada like a cat burglar searching for a point of entry.

My brother Charles tracked me down through adoption records, and when we met he introduced me to traditional people. There was an elder he'd been travelling with who had an entourage of followers keen on learning traditional Ojibway spirituality. I'd never met traditional people before, and the idea of Indian ceremony was fraught with anxiety for me.

Back then I thought that you had to qualify as native, Indian, Ojibway. I thought people were measured by the Indian-ness they wore on their sleeve. Nothing about me measured up in that regard.

But they welcomed me. I was greeted kindly and made to feel included. They knew that I was one of the lost ones, one of the disappeared ones who were slowly making their way back to their original homes, their original territories, their original way of being. They understood the difficulty in that, and they tried their best to make the transition easier for me.

Still I was anxious, and when I was invited to a ceremony I wanted to run the other way. Everything I'd heard of native ceremony was built on superstition and fear. I'd heard gossip about shape-shifters, bad spirits, Bear Walkers and hallucinatory visions. I'd heard of bad medicine, and I was fearful that my lack of anything remotely resembling Ojibway would set me up for the black powers.

What I found was the opposite.

We gathered in a circle in someone's living room. We sat respectfully while the elder prepared, and as I looked around at the faces of those people I was struck by their calm. As one of the apprentices began to make his way around the circle with a large abalone bowl that held a pile of smouldering herbs, we all stood.

The elder explained that we would purify ourselves with the smoke from that bowl. We would pass it over ourselves, smudge ourselves, to cleanse the detritus of living from our minds, emotions, bodies and spirits. In this way, he said, we would return ourselves to the innocence in which we were born, the humility that is the foundation of everything.

We are watched over, he said. Always. We are guided and protected by our grandmothers and grandfathers in the Spirit World, our ancestors, the Old Ones who love us regardless. The smoke as it rises from the bowl carries our thoughts, feelings and prayers to the Spirit World, where they are heard.

I watched as others smudged, and when it came my turn I did as they had done. I passed the smoke over my head and over my heart, the smell of it pungent and sweet, an old smell, ancient and comforting. When I closed my eyes to pass the smoke over my head again I found the silence I'd been searching for all my life.

There was only breath in it. There was only the slow beating of my heart like a drum in the darkness, and the presence of something warm, safe and eternal wafting around my shoulders, lifting me, cocooning me, sheltering me. There was only the feel of hands, wrinkled and lined by time, softened by rest and calm, that touched my face and offered comfort.

In the depths of that incredible silence I knew there was more to me than I'd ever dreamed. I'd never needed to qualify, to prove myself worthy. I was Ojibway, I was Indian, and I was home.

Man Walking by the Crooked Water

. . .

MY GRANDFATHER'S NAME was John Wagamese. Our family name comes from an Ojibway phrase meaning "man walking by the crooked water." It was shortened by the treaty registrar because Wagamese was all he could pronounce of it, but the name came from the trapline my great-great-grandfather established along the Winnipeg River. My grandfather walked it all his life.

He was a bush man, John Wagamese. There was nothing he didn't know of it, couldn't comprehend or predict. The land was as much a part of him as his skin, and he wore it proudly, humbly and with much honour. In our patch of northern Ontario, north of Lake of the Woods, he was a legend. People still talk about how strong he was. He carried a moose carcass ten miles out of the bush one time, and on another occasion he fashioned a harness from the canvas of his tent and hauled 120 pounds of blueberries a day's walk to the northern store for sale. He knew every inch of our traditional territory, and in my mind I see him walking it—a man walking by the crooked water.

My grandfather's life was the last truly traditional one in my family history. He never learned to speak English, never learned to read or write, never had a driver's licence, but he knew the land like an old hymn. It sang through him, wild and exuberant and free.

There's a picture of us in my mother's photo album. I'm young with long hair, trying as hard as I can to look the part of the Indian. My grandfather is sitting on a bed in light-blue pajamas, his nose bent from being broken, eyes sparkling above the fists of cheekbone beneath his wind-wrinkled skin, his hair in a severe brush cut and his bush man's hands clasped almost shyly in his lap. There was never a question about who the real Indian in that photo is.

I met him when I was twenty-five. I'd never even known I had a grandfather. The arthritis had confined John to a nursing home by then, and I went to see him whenever I could. When I entered his room for the first time, he looked at me with a toothless smile. He held his hand out at about the height of a small child, nodded and welcomed me home. I've never forgotten that—how strong the language of love can be.

Through an interpreter, I asked my grandfather questions about our history, about our traditions, about the world he knew in the bush. He was generous, and he loved to talk. As he did the land came alive for him again. In his mind's eye he was the young man of local legend, striding through the bush filled with purpose. Now and then I'd sneak him in a beer or two. He'd sip them and tell me about the old days.

My world was foreign to my grandfather, and hearing him talk of times when simplicity was a virtue and independence meant always mending your own net, I learned how foreign that life was to me. But it was mine, accorded to me by history, by family, by the recollections of an old man wearied some by the trail and eager to pass on his stories.

I became an Indian at twenty-five because of John Wagamese. I still had the long hair, the beaded vest, the moccasins, the turquoise rings, the Hollywood trappings of the Indian that I'd taken on in my city life, but I wanted the Indian look I saw in that photo of my grandfather. A look that said, "All that I am is here." In the years since, I've sometimes been fortunate enough to feel it on my face.

My grandfather died in his sleep the year I was thirty-two. When I heard the news I lay in my bed and stared at the sky outside my window for a long time. I wasn't sad for him. His life had been a celebration. I wasn't bitter and I wasn't angry. What he had given me I could never lose.

To honour my grandfather, I took a walk out on the land. Standing there, looking out across the broad sweep of the country he loved, what I felt for him was everything, love and joy and grief and loss. I knew that feeling had an Ojibway name, but I hadn't found the language for it yet.

A Raven Tale

. . .

MY PEOPLE TELL a story about a raven who dreamed of eagles.

It seems a young raven grew fascinated with the majestic flight of those great warrior birds. To this young raven, eagles were immaculate creations. When he looked at the stubbiness of his own wings, he was dissatisfied. When he examined the sooty black of his feathers, he felt ugly and ill-defined. He wanted more than anything to soar and to feel the admiration of his fellow ravens. Every day he watched the eagles drift over the pine tree where he sat, and every day he dreamed of being an eagle.

One day this young raven began to practise soaring. He leapt from his perch in the pine tree and held his wings out straight and aimed for the highest branch of a neighbouring tree. It wasn't that far, but he wavered in the air. Still, he made it. The young raven felt huge.

Every day after that he flapped to a private part of the forest to practise. He disappeared, alone, to work on increasing his strength and his range. He got stronger. He grew better able to hold the air in his short black feathers. His flights began to feel long and elegant. He could bank and turn and spiral in weightless glides across the roof of his forest world. But it wasn't enough. He needed to be seen. So one day, when he was sitting in a clutch of his fellow ravens, the young raven took off. While they watched he flapped higher and higher. They called to him to come back, but he climbed and climbed until he was a small black dot in the sky. Then he began to soar.

He held out his stubby wings and felt the currents of the air. As he banked into a lazy spiral, he could see his family and friends below flapping about in excitement. No raven had ever soared before. No raven had ever come close to being an eagle. He felt incredible pride, and he banked even more steeply to show off his new-found power.

But raven wings are not meant for soaring, and he tired quickly. Far above the ground he fought hard to hold the air. He trembled. He wavered. He shook. He grew fearful. The world began to spin. The long spiral became a crazy spin. His friends watched in horror as the young raven dropped like a stone from the sky.

Well, lucky for him, he crashed into the highest branches of his favourite pine tree. The heavy limbs broke his fall as he tumbled through them. Finally, he landed with a thud on the ground at the pine tree's roots. He was bedraggled and dazed, missing a lot of feathers, but he was alive.

Later, he told a wise old raven about his adventure. He told her how he'd dreamed of being an eagle and had been dissatisfied with his lot in life as a raven. She listened, then sat for a long while considering his words.

We're all born with gifts. That's what she told him, finally. As the eagle is blessed, so too are the ravens. That's the truth of the world. The trick is to seek out your own gifts, make use of them and learn to soar in that way.

That young raven paid attention to the Old One's words. He stayed closer to the ground after that and began to accept himself as a raven. He discovered many marvellous things, developed exciting skills and abilities. As he grew he passed those on to younger ravens. But he never forgot the lesson in his dreams of eagles.

That's why, to this day, when you watch a raven fly you will see it flap, flap and then soar.

WHEN I HEARD that story for the first time, I thought it was a charming little folk tale. It called to mind campfires, sparkly-eyed children, dark nights, a hand drum and the drone of an old storyteller's voice. I didn't realize it was an appropriate and timely teaching.

It was the early 1980s, and I was trying hard to make it in radio. I worked as a newscaster on the old CKO All News network in Calgary. I spent all my spare time listening to the other radio newscasters, and every night I practised trying to sound like them, bringing their ebullient, professional timbre into my own delivery.

I got good, but every newscast was a huge effort.

Trying to sound like those I admired made reading the news twice the work. When I got a job with CBC Radio a year or so later, my trainer listened to me a while, then told me to quit working so hard. Just be myself, she advised. I'd read better and sound more genuine.

Well, she was right. We had a successful program on CBC. I went on to work at a few major market stations and eventually became a program director at one of the first native stations in the country. All by being myself and using my own gifts.

That's the trick of it in this life. There are a million shiny things around us, and it's easy to get distracted. Drink it all in, but make it your own. Find your own chunk of the sky, then flap, flap, soar. Flap, flap, soar.

Shooting Trudeau

· · ·

WHEN THE SUN shoots through the gap that
forms the green *V* of these mountains, it becomes a spot-
light. It picks out particular stands of trees on the far shore
of the lake, and sometimes it catches a clutch of ducks, the
paddling ring of them iridescent.

My people call it *wash-ko-nah-shpee-ming*—light in
the sky. There are legends told of it and teachings accorded
to its properties. In traditional times, those days before set-
tlement, spiritual societies gathered to welcome the light's
arrival each morning.

For me, this is meditation time. The dog and I walk the
lakefront and marvel at the light that makes things so new
and different each day. Some people are like that, too. They
seem to rearrange the particles of air around them, letting
you see ordinary things in new and luminous ways.

I met one such man in the spring of 1983.

I was thirteen when Pierre Trudeau came to power
in 1968. Earlier that year, I'd watched on television as he
snared the Liberal leadership after four votes. When he
became prime minister, riding on a wave of Trudeaumania,
I was caught up. He was a rebel, and part of me responded
to that, just as it did to the charismatic bon vivant.

I knew little of politics then. I didn't know how the Canadian model of federalism affected my life as a native person. But I did know a poverty of the spirit, and whenever light broke through the opaqueness of my world, I leaned towards it hungrily. Pierre Trudeau, with the gallant rose in his lapel, the whirl of girlfriends, the sports cars and the vaunted intellectual *savoir faire*, was a shimmering beacon of hope for me. When he invoked the *War Measures Act* in the face of FLQ insurrection, I imagined him a modern knight in defence of the realm.

I had no idea about the 1969 White Paper on Indian policy and its proposed destruction of all things Aboriginal. I had no clue about the intentions of the Indian Affairs minister, Jean Chretien, and his prime minister. If I'd been more aware of these things, I might have had a far different image of Trudeau, the man. But politics for me then bore no colour.

I became a journalist in 1978, the year before Trudeau was defeated by Joe Clark. When Trudeau returned to power and began rattling the sabre of constitutional change, I watched carefully. I'd become more astute by then, understood how government worked and how its rhythms affected me and my people. Bringing the Constitution back to Canada, wresting it away from the Crown, was a significant breach of the trust surrounding treaties, which had been signed "the Crown in the right of Great Britain." The act was as brutal in its way as the White

Paper had been, and Indians crossed the ocean in waves to appeal to the British House of Lords and the Royal Family. Notwithstanding, Trudeau and the Queen signed the document over to Canada in 1982.

In March of 1983, Indians were invited to meet with the provincial First Ministers and the Government of Canada to haggle over their representation in the new Constitution. Delegations of us travelled to Ottawa to see history made. I was one of the hundred or so journalists covering the event. For me, with a Grade Nine education and a history of homelessness and poverty, to sit in a press room with the leading journalists of my time was unbelievable.

The biggest thrill was the press conference on the second day. My organization, Saskatchewan Native Communications, was on the list of questioners, and we had grabbed seats in the front row. The editor of the newsmagazine, Joan Beatty, was too nervous to take photos or to ask questions when our turn came, so I did it. While Trudeau fielded questions from the gallery I snapped a whole roll of film. Crouching, leaning, aiming my wide angle and zoom, I photographed the man I'd seen as such a symbol of bold individuality in my youth. My shot of Trudeau leaning forward, cupping a hand to his ear to hear a question, later became the newsmagazine's cover photo.

When I stood to pose the three questions I'd prepared, I felt a fire spring to life within me. For five minutes I stood face to face with greatness and held my own. He fielded my questions with dignity, nodding in recognition of their value. He answered respectfully, learnedly. I wasn't just an Indian that day. I was a journalist, and I deserved his attention. When I sat back down I allowed myself to breathe again.

That was the day I knew I qualified as a journalist. When Trudeau looked at me, I knew I mattered. Seven years later, accepting a National Newspaper Award, I thanked him silently.

Pierre Trudeau was a hero of mine. I'm not ashamed to say that now, despite the politics. Some people are a light in the sky. They chase shadow from your world and grant you vision. *Ahow.*

The Medicine Wheel

. . .

THE RAIN IS a fine sprinkle on the trees this
morning. When the sun pokes its head through the thin
cloud, there's a happy conjunction of energy everywhere
around. The land breathes, and I can almost feel the huff of
it, the great lungs of Mother Earth receiving and releasing.
A rainbow links the mountains. Beneath its layered
parabola birds wheel and dive. There are teachings in all
of this. I walk here to make myself available to them, but
it wasn't always that way. It took a special man to help
me see the necessity.

His name was Cliff Thompson. He was a huge bear of
a man who laughed easily and loud, and he was a spiritual
teacher from the Sioux tradition. A group of us were in
the Qu'Appelle Valley in southern Saskatchewan, surrounded by sand cliffs, water, sage hills and rangeland as
far as the eye could see. Cliff was teaching us about the
native way of seeing the world.

When he spoke you could feel his passion. He talked of
sun dances and spiritual ceremonies he'd been blessed to
take part in. He spoke of the elders who'd graced him with
teachings and of how his life had changed as a result. He

spoke about the land as if it were a loved one, family, kin. The brown of him, his skin, his eyes, radiated affection.

On the second night we gathered in a darkened room. Candles were burning, and the sweet smell of burnt sage filled the air. In the centre of the room Cliff had set up an altar. It was round, the lines of it drawn by hand. It was painted in what I'd learned were the colours of the four cardinal directions. There were stones on it, roots, a pine cone, eagle feathers, a wooden bowl of water, a swatch of deer hide, antlers, a hand drum and a red stone ceremonial pipe. In the hushed lighting of the candles, the altar seemed to breathe. None of us spoke. We were awed by the quiet power of those articles, and we sat humbly awaiting the teachings.

He sang a song with the drum. He prayed, then asked us to stand while he smudged us with the sacred smoke from an abalone bowl, using a huge eagle-wing fan. We sat again, and he closed his eyes and breathed. The energy in the room unsettled me some, this huge fibrillation of power all around me.

When he began to speak the flicker of the candles lent his words a timeless feel. Closing my eyes, I could imagine myself back a thousand years with that same light dancing on the skin of a teepee, the land hushed around us.

He spoke of the Medicine Wheel. There were no flip charts, handouts, diagrams or detailed texts, just the power of his words. This was the way the teachings were offered in traditional times, each person discerning what they could and carrying it with them.

As Cliff talked, I opened up. Within the great wheel of energy, he said, everything is related. Our journey is many journeys, because everything we do affects something or someone else. Learning to travel with dignity, with humility and with respect for the creative energy in all things is the heart of the Indian way. That's what he taught us.

There is life force in everything. Everything is alive, animate, moving and, even if we can't see that, we can learn to feel it. When we do, we come to true awareness of our ongoing state of relationship. That awareness lies beyond the brain. We feel it in our spirits, our hearts. It is there that the teachings live and learning occurs.

"Medicine" is a sacred word, "something that joins you to the world." The Medicine Wheel is a process of coming to know your feelings. Learning to travel with your feelings as your guide is an arduous journey that few have the courage to make. Knowing and wisdom, though, can come only from that trek. Simple truths shine in the sun of every new morning. The world awaits us.

Coming to Beedahbun

. . .

THE MOON on the water is a pale eye. It hangs suspended, like a dream upon awakening. The lake bears it effortlessly, and the scrim of trees along the skyline thrust up like fingers to tickle its belly. You'd swear you can hear the chuckle of it against the morning adagio of shorebirds. My people call this time of day *Beedahbun*, first light. In traditional times, Ojibway medicine societies gathered in the vesperal quiet for prayer and ceremony. They gathered to celebrate the light in the sky. Those morning rituals were a celebration of energy, a recognition of the harmony we often live in so blindly. For me now, it's meditative time. I feel Ojibway standing at the edge of a mountain lake watching eagles and ospreys soar and dive.

I discovered the whole *Beedahbun* thing one glorious week in the autumn of 1985. I was struggling to survive then. My first marriage had ended badly, and I found myself sleeping on my mother's couch. I was drinking too much, to try to kill the pain of it, and it took a while to get my feet under me again.

Northern Ontario in early fall is a spectacle. There's a change happening all around you. When you take the time, you can see it in the animals, in the plants and trees, on the face of the water. I'd found a job as a marina helper on the Winnipeg River, and I sat every morning watching the sun break over the water. While I drank coffee and waited for the first boatloads of fishermen to arrive, I let myself fall into the lap of those mornings. In the heat of the day, when the fishermen napped, I sat under a huge pine tree at the edge of the bay and tried to write.

The words that formed in me were melancholic, aching words that assembled themselves as poetry. I'd always felt my strength was the straight-ahead clarity of journalism. The few poems I'd tried up to that point were sentimental and heavy-handed. But something clicked under that pine tree. It heartened me and eased my pain. When the *Wawatay News* in Sioux Lookout agreed to print my poems, I was thrilled.

A man named Simon Frog read those poems in the paper. Simon was cultural development officer for the Nishnawbe Aski Nation, and he was working with Ojibway elders to encourage native youth to write, to tell the stories of their people, to continue the grand line of storytellers. He had a workshop set up on Manitoulin Island at a place called Beedahbun Lodge, and when he read my poetry he wanted me to take part in it. Naturally, I agreed.

There were a handful of us at the workshop. Some were from remote reserves like Kasabonika Lake, Big Trout Lake and Lac Brochet, Manitoba. Others, like me, were from the cities. We were guided by a pair of published poets, Paulette Jiles and Robert Bringhurst, and a dozen Ojibway elders from across the Nishnawbe Aski territory.

Every day we spoke with the elders and heard amazing traditional stories. Then we went to work. We brainstormed ideas, looking for a mix of the traditional and the contemporary, a symbiosis. We workshopped a number of things and one, a delightful theatre piece in which we built a talking human totem pole, was greeted with thunderous applause from the elders.

I heard the *Beedahbun* teaching there. Every day I was up early, stepping out of the lodge to walk in the energy of morning. I looked for the joining, the blending the elders had told us of. It healed me when I found it, I was able to create spontaneously for the first time, and I walked away from that week-long retreat determined to become a storyteller.

Others left determined to create too. Tomson Highway went on to write *The Rez Sisters* and other acclaimed plays. Billy Merasty became a successful actor. Shirley Cheechoo is now a fine film director and me, well, I'm a writer with many more stories yet to see the light of day.

I still come to observe *Beedahbun*. Every morning, regardless of the season, I'm out early, walking in silence, opening myself to the mystery one more time. It never gets old. It never gets boring. It's never the same way twice. The land works a subtle magic, and it's in subtlety that the teaching comes. First light breaking. Shadow eased from the world. Spirit energy, in us, in the land, in the universe.

Thunder Teachings

. . .

WHEN THE THUNDER rolls through these
mountains, you feel it long before you hear it. We're up
high enough here that the air is a messenger. Standing on
the deck, my skin a barometer, I feel the advance chill of a
storm, then the dip in pressure like the lurch of an elevator.
It's not like the storms I remember as a kid. There's no
frightening clap to send you scurrying to your bed, the
closet, the nearest adult. Instead, you feel a smug sense of
satisfaction as you wait for it. It's as if you've become a part
of the mountains yourself. As the storm moves across the
lake, birds fall silent and the dog raises her snout, scenting
the cordite snap of lightning in the roar.

Maybe it's the Ojibway in me that is moved by this
experience. Maybe there's something in the traditional
genes I carry that recalls the ancient teachings borne in the
voice of the sky. Thunder Beings, spirit teachers flapping in
on gigantic wings to illuminate, enlighten. Or maybe it's
simply the majestic, sonic beauty of it all.

My people say the time of the first thunders is a sacred
time. When thunder rumbles for the first time in spring,
there are certain medicines to gather, sacred herbs that
absorb the punch of it and become empowered for healing.

Thunder is the sign of life force returning after the lethargy of winter. There are dances and ceremonies, prayer songs and rituals to celebrate it.

When I was in my thirties I was invited to the opening of a Sacred Bundle, the Beaver Bundle of the Peigan people in southern Alberta. The bundle is opened after the first thunders are heard, and you must be invited in order to attend. Bundle keepers are particular about who is around when the sacred items in the bundle are exposed.

I was working closely with a traditional elder then and moving in traditional tribal circles. I had a regular column in a native newspaper and produced a native newsmagazine program for a Calgary TV station. But when I was invited to the bundle opening, I felt more honoured than I had ever been.

A Sacred Bundle is the medicine power of the people. Within it are objects valued for their spiritual integrity and their ability to transfer vital energy. The ancient prayers, songs and rituals performed at the opening are meant to re-energize the bundle and prepare us for the spiritual work we will do over the next four seasons. There are prayers at dawn and dusk. The sacred pipe is smoked, and there are rituals around each of the elements of the bundle that can't be spoken of or written about.

On the journey to the ceremony I was reflective and calm. The land seemed sharper in detail, and there was a solemnity to everything, so that a red-tailed hawk skimming over the front of the car took on an immense significance. I wondered at the appearance of coyotes and deer and crows. The land and its inhabitants seemed prepared for a time of union.

The gathering was small. There were about twenty of us from a variety of backgrounds, traditional reserve-based people, urban Indians and a few non-native friends of the bundle keeper. What we shared was a deep respect for ceremony and its role in the health and well-being of our communities.

When the ceremony began, a sense of sanctity was alive in the air. I can't say much about the nature of that ceremony. I can say only that each element of the bundle was presented, prayed over, sung for and praised. I can say only that every one of those sacred objects was treated reverentially, and being in their presence was elevating. Their power presented itself as fully as thunder rolling over a mountain. I walked away filled with a sense of wonder.

The opening of a Sacred Bundle is a returning. It cuts through the modern trappings of our lives and releases us into the elemental spiritual way. The truth is, we all have Sacred Bundles. They are our memories, our stories, our learning on this journey. They are everything we hold as special, as holy, as timeless. Each part is vital because it helps make us who we are. Opening up and sharing them is a ceremony in its purest sense. That's true for all of us, Indian or not.

Vanishing Points

. . .

MY PEOPLE SAY that there are seven hills to
life. Each hill is a vantage point for looking back, though
not everyone takes the time for reflection.

There is a hill for youth and adolescence, a hill for
adulthood and parenting. There are the hills of middle life,
the teaching time, and on into the elder years, the giving-
back time. The Ojibway say it is only in looking back that
you discern the trail, identify the climb and rest contented
in each stage of the journey. The final hill is the eleva-
tion of wisdom. From there you can look back on the vast
panorama of your life and come to know who you are by
virtue of who you've been.

In the summer of 1987, I sat on a ledge of rock in
the mountains of Montana with a young Blackfoot elder.
We were part of a traditional gathering called Return to
the Buffalo. We camped in a sacred meadow where people
of many nations had gathered in pre-settlement times
to share teachings and earth knowledge. Like then, the
members of our group came from diverse cultures, and the
time we shared there was built entirely on the true tribal
way of life.

The view from that ledge was amazing. The mountains around us formed a perfect bowl, a circle that seemed to contain everything. Across the gap of valley was a turquoise lake. The trees were a hundred shades of green, the sky a blue that pulled your gaze upwards and away and back again. The view itself was ceremony. I was crying. The experience of living the tribal way was what I had been searching out for years.

We'd been separated into clans, and each of us had been given responsibility for parts of daily life. I was Beaver Clan, and we were responsible for firewood and watching over the children. There were traditional teachings about these responsibilities, and we'd gather under an arbour to hear them. I came to understand community there, came to know what unity looked like, how harmony could feel.

Every night we sat in a round lodge and listened to the elders. We learned sacred songs on hand drums, heard stories, asked questions and were taught according to traditional protocol.

The experience was moving and fulfilling. But it was time to go. Soon we'd head out, scattered across the Four Directions to wherever our homes were, and the likelihood of gathering together again in that way was slim. I was heartbroken. But it was time to go.

We sat on that ledge for a long time as I told the young teacher how much this time had meant to me and how it hurt to see it end. He listened intently. When I had finished he looked across that sweep of valley. Then he told me about the seven hills, as it had been told to him by an Ojibway shaman.

Nothing is ever truly lost, he said. Everything exists on energy, invisible and eternal. The highest form that energy takes is feeling. The heart has no questions, he said, and the head has no answers. Our heads tell us to believe in finalities, endings, but nothing is ever truly lost.

The hills of life are resting spots, he told me. You only come to know that when you take the time to look back. Then you discover that everything you carry lives in you as feeling. We are in constant relationship with everything, he said, and relationships never end. They merely change.

Take this place with you, he told me. Breathe it into you. Someday you'll unwrap it and see it like it was, perfectly, truly. On that day, he said, you'll see that there are no vanishing points. You can see forever from those hills, and you will never be lonely.

I've forgotten his teaching from time to time, as we all allow the sublime things in life to fade. But when I remember it, during times that are tough or unclear, I realize yet again that the climb has been worth it. The view is spectacular from here.

The Beetle Trees

. . .

AGAINST THE FLANK of mountain, red pine trees wither. As the pine beetles eat their way through the forest, the trees become incapable of moving water from their roots. You can hear them die in the relentless hurtling of needles to the ground. The cones drop heavily, roll sullenly to a stop. Even the wind has changed tone, keening as it passes through the branches.

In our yard we're losing five pine trees. We fought hard to save them. We've sprayed, applied Verbenone patches, watered and fed them. Those trees are all over a hundred years old, stately and refined. When they go we'll be lessened, a clear-cut path through the soul.

A pine tree gave me an important teaching once. It was the late 1980s, and I was in the forest with Jack Kakakaway. Jack was a veteran, a well-respected elder and powwow dancer. He'd survived a war and alcoholism and despair. He'd transcended racism and bigotry. He was rooted, settled, with a big laugh and a wild sense of humour.

I'd come to Jack with questions, and he would point me in the right direction. He would never tell me something outright. He'd allow me to find my own path to the answer that was right for me. If I stumbled along the way, he was always there to encourage, affirm and validate my efforts. He was a great friend and a tremendous teacher. That day we were in the foothills gathering rocks for a sweat lodge ceremony. As we wandered through the trees, he talked about the Plant People and the teaching that trees are grandfathers and grandmothers with stories to tell if we learn to listen. He pointed to a large oak tree nearly clear of leaves. It stood on a hillside against the hard blue sky. Trees are more like us than we realize, he said. He pointed to the oak's limbs and branches and shoots. They are like the network of veins and capillaries in our bodies, he said. Trees are alive, have a spirit, a history, and much to say to us.

He told me to go for a walk. When I came across a big old tree that appealed to me, I was to sit under it, lean against the trunk and listen. There would be a teaching for me there if I was patient enough to hear it. So I left him and began to roam through that foothills forest.

I found an old ponderosa pine that was tall and wide with thick roots that anchored it in the hardscrabble earth. There was a natural cleft in the spread of roots, and I settled in and leaned back. At first I stared upwards at the branches, watching the clouds through them. Then I closed my eyes and breathed, long and deep. I could feel the bark of the tree against my back and the slight sway of it in the wind.

I leaned my head back and listened. It was the tail end of summer, and I could hear the rustle of leaves around me. Beyond that I heard the bawl of cattle on the rangeland a half mile below. There was traffic noise from the highway a long way off, and the sound of a jet somewhere to the south. In the trees I heard songbirds and, higher, the screech of a hawk.

Then I listened for the sounds of the tree itself. There was a soughing of wind through the branches. A squirrel skittered along a limb. A bird twittered. A pine cone clattered branch to branch. Nearer the top I heard the claws of a porcupine or raccoon against the bark. But the harder I tried to focus, the more my mind wandered.

Then, as I struggled to maintain my attention, I heard a voice. It said, very softly, "Shh." That's all. Shh. Grand-motherly, grandfatherly. Calming. Soothing. Settling. Shh. Be still.

I must have sat under that tree for a few hours, with my eyes closed. When I opened them and went to find Jack I felt rested, filled with energy and a sense of peace. When I told Jack this and asked him what the teaching was, he only smiled and said that it would come to me.

It did.

Jack passed away nearly sixteen years ago. He was leading a sweat lodge ceremony for inmates at a federal prison when he had a fatal heart attack. Even at the end he was giving, teaching, leading. When I heard I went out and listened to the trees.

It may have been only the wind I heard that day, the empty part of me reaching out for contact with my history, my people, my tribal self. But back then I needed to believe that there were voices in the trees, grandmothers and grandfathers with something vital to say. And the truth is that there are.

The web of life is a fragile thing, and every strand is necessary. If we believe that the voices of our ancestors speak to us through the trees, we will fight to protect them. Standing here, watching my friends die, I know that it's the struggle to protect life that saves us. The beetle trees will stand as a symbol of what we gained through the struggle, not what we lost. Shh. Be quiet. Be still.

IN THE MOUNTAINS the night sky is startlingly
near. Darkness falls gradually here, and the first poke of
stars over the southern ridge is cool as ice against the
fading heat of the day. From our deck you feel pressed up
against the sky as the rest of the stars emerge.

I love the sky. I always have. Friends sometimes have
wondered at my tendency to gaze up at it during gaps in
our conversation. "Like you're waiting for the words to
fall," someone said one time, and he was far more accurate
than he realized.

In the summer of 1989 I took a day trip with two
friends into the foothills of southern Alberta. The drive
out was wonderful. Van Morrison sang on the CD player,
the windows were down and the coffee was hot and strong.

We drove to an area where the Sheep River tumbles out
of the mountains. There's a small falls, and we picnicked
on the flat rocks at the side of it. After a spell of reading,
drawing or simply looking at the landscape, we hiked along
a trail that meandered beside the river.

Brian was a gifted fingerstyle guitar player who'd once
lived in a tree house with a Cajun girl in Louisiana. During
the Summer of Love he'd hitchhiked across the country

with a cello. He'd been to Spain and France and Greece, and we had long conversations about everything from Dvořák and Son House to Marx and postmodern literature.

Kathy was a Maritimer who'd grown up in Saint John, New Brunswick. She was a small-town girl at heart, old-fashioned and loyal, with an insatiable curiosity about the world. She was an artist, or working hard at becoming one. She was tall, brown-eyed and beautiful, worn down some by the moves of men. She and I had tried to be lovers, but we were better suited as friends.

Each of us was in pursuit of a dream. For Brian it was a life of fulfillment through art and music. Kathy craved a home, a family, stability. Me, I was seeking definition as a native man and had vague hopes of writing, publishing, creating. It was our dreams that brought us together.

When evening came we found a firepit in a camp-ground and prepared supper. None of us wanted to leave. As darkness fell, we began to tell a shared story around the fire. Each of us would tell part of it, then pass the story on to another who continued the thread. The story, about a man who got lost in the jungle, was vivid and wonderful.

It was late by the time we felt motivated to move. When the fire was doused, the darkness was complete, and we could feel the raw power of the land all around us. We walked wordlessly across the parking lot to the car. Driving out of the mountains, we kept the windows down so we could see the stars.

We'd just slid out onto the gentle roll of the grasslands when Brian told me to stop. After I pulled the car over he jumped out and ran a few steps into the field, gazing upwards at the sky. We joined him.

What we saw in that night sky was unforgettable. They were lights, four, maybe five, orange and red and yellow. As they moved across the sky, you could tell that they were closer than the stars. They changed directions. They changed speeds. Their brightness altered, and when they came together suddenly in a tight formation, then disappeared at supersonic speed, we heaved a collective breath. The sky was stiller, emptier, than before.

We sat there for a long time, wanting them to reappear. But they never did. Instead, the sky became a panorama of galaxies, planets and constellations. We watched it until our yawns signalled our need to be home. We didn't speak for the rest of that drive. There were no words to describe what we'd seen.

Brian eventually disappeared in the direction of Montreal, and Kathy found her man and home and permanence. We haven't seen each other in years. But somewhere, I know, they both look at the stars and remember that night. We're all Star People. We're all part of the cosmos, and the air we share is the first breath of Creation. That means we can never be separate. We're kin, and sometimes it takes magic to show us that.

Two Skunks

. . .

WHEN I WAS in my late thirties I travelled to Temagami, Ontario, to attend a retreat for native men who had experienced cultural dislocation. We spent ten days reconnecting to traditional ways and teachings, guided by a team of elders and healers. Most of us were city dwellers, used to the pace of urban life. Most of us did not speak our language. None of us had ever directly faced the issues of our displacement.

As soon as we arrived we were paired up in tents. My tent mate, Paul, was a thirty-nine-year-old half-Cree man who'd been born in northern Quebec. He lived in Montreal, worked there as a pastry chef and had hardly been outside the city. Like me, he had been taken away from his people as a toddler. Unlike me, he had been in more than twenty foster homes by the time he was sixteen. He'd come to the camp to begin the journey back to tribal identity.

The first day of sessions we were asked to choose an animal name for the length of our stay. We were to tell the group why we had chosen that animal. I called myself Wandering Bear. I said that I admired the bear for his ability to live alone for great lengths of time, yet still enjoy family and togetherness.

When it came to Paul's turn, he said that he was a skunk. He sat with his head down, staring at the ground, clasping and unclasping his fingers. He said he'd chosen a skunk because they're scavengers, rooting around for whatever they can find.

"What's lower than a skunk?" he asked.

"I don't know," one of the guides replied. "Two?"

From that day on Paul was Two Skunks.

In those ten days we learned to build fires without paper or matches. We learned to set gillnets, clean fish, shoot rapids in a canoe, snare rabbits, read animal tracks and make bows and arrows in the traditional manner. We each spent a night alone in the bush, building lean-tos from spruce boughs. We learned about the spiritual way that guided all those practices.

There were sweat lodge ceremonies, prayer and smudging circles, tobacco offerings, drumming circles and a lot of talk. Each of us spoke about growing up without a native identity. We shared stories of awkwardness, the struggle to fit in. We talked of where our trails had taken us and how we felt about where we'd been.

Two Skunks spoke so quietly we had to strain to hear him. Over the course of days he told us about the sexual abuse he'd suffered at the hands of a foster father. He'd never spent a whole year in any one home. When he was sixteen, old enough to be on his own, he went to the streets of Montreal. He sold himself there, to men. He drank and drugged. He stole and went to prison, where he sold himself again to survive.

He talked of hating his skin. He spoke of wanting sometimes to scrape it off. He felt betrayed by it. No one had given him any answers about where he came from, who his people were or who he was supposed to be. He spoke of never feeling honest or deserving or worthy. He spoke of the hole at the centre of his being.

But the elders took him in hand. They held healing ceremonies for him, which we all got to attend. They gave him permission to cry about it all, and he did. In the sweat lodge he prayed hard for the ability to forgive himself. Then he prayed for the forgiveness of those who had hurt him. At nights we talked quietly in our tent, and he spoke of the incredible feeling of light that was beginning to shine in him.

One day, he asked me to come along with him and an elder. We walked deep into the bush where Two Skunks made tobacco offerings and gave thanks for everything that had happened in his life. He thanked the universe for the gifts of those teachings. Then he put those offerings in the ground, returning them to earth, and sang a prayer song. I felt honoured to be there.

When the retreat was over we hugged and went our separate ways. He wrote me sporadically through the years. He joined a drum group in Montreal, started to learn his language and attended Talking Circles and sweat lodges every week. He wrote about feeling happy, about being connected, about finally feeling Indian.

Then one day a letter arrived from a woman who said she was Paul's wife. She was Cree. They'd been married four years and had a young daughter named Rain. Two Skunks had died of complications from diabetes. He was only forty-four. But he'd become a traditional dancer and singer. He'd helped guide a traditional camp in her community, and he spoke his language fluently. When he died he was buried in the traditional way.

I sat with that letter in my hands for a long time. Then I went deep into the bush, returned it to earth and gave thanks for the teaching.

We heal each other by sharing the stories of our time here. We heal each other through love. In the Indian way, that means you leading me back to who I am. There's no bigger gift, and all it takes is listening and hearing. *Ahow.*

Bringing Back the Living Room

· · ·

IN OUR HOME NOW, the television is hardly
ever on. There's something about having the open land a
step away that makes TV irrelevant. We watch the news,
have our favourite couple of programs and I catch all the
baseball games I can. But mainly, our TV is the picture
window that looks out over the lake.

At night, walking with the dog down the gravel road,
we can see many of our neighbours huddled in a ghostly
blue glow. We return to our living room to read, talk and
listen to music, everything from John Legend to Kitty
Wells to Ravel and Buddy Guy. When the lights are low,
that's what we prefer.

In the winter of 1991, I got to meet Johnny Cash. I was
an entertainment writer for the *Calgary Herald* then, but
it wasn't because of that I got to speak with him. It was
because I was a native person. I wrote cultural columns for
native papers. I'd sent the record company reps a handful of
them and asked to talk to John when he came to town. He
read them and agreed.

Johnny Cash was always concerned with the lives of
native people. In 1964 he'd recorded an eight-song album

called *Bitter Tears (Ballads of the American Indian)*. That ballad was a sad one, John said, and his songs reflected that. The "Ballad of Ira Hayes," "Drums" and "The Vanishing Race" were powerful songs directing the listener to the plight of the Indian in contemporary North America. Only country music fans know those songs, except for the Hayes tune. But John was never far from the cause of native rights. When he read my pieces he wanted to talk informally, off the record, to learn more about the native experience in this country.

We met in his hotel room. He was passing through on a tour with the Carter Family, and though I'd review the concert for the paper, we agreed that our conversation was not to be used. As it turned out, I couldn't have done it justice.

The occasion sits in me like a dream. I was guided into the living room of his suite and he walked in, tall, angular, his hair still black and combed back, his obsidian eyes intelligent and soulful. He shook my hand warmly and said the famous words: "Hello, I'm Johnny Cash." Then he sat down across from me and we began to talk.

I told him about my life, my family's tragic history and the joys and pains of reconnecting to my native identity. I told him about land claims, treaty rights, racism, bigotry, the ongoing work that's required for a people to emancipate themselves. He nodded lots and asked pointed, articulate questions.

Eventually, he made his questions personal. He asked me how I felt about all those issues. He asked me how it felt to be in my skin every day. He asked me what dreams I had for myself and how hard they might be to realize as a native person in Canada. And he asked what I would change about myself if I could.

We talked about ceremony and spirituality. We talked of sweat lodges, sun dances, sacred pipes and prayer songs. We talked about the land and how allowing it to seep inside you is such a transcendent experience it is nearly impossible to express. He was an Indian, Johnny Cash, if not in blood then in sentiment and spirit.

He told me about the early influence of gospel on his music. He talked about the teachings he'd gleaned and how, in the end, returning to them saved his life. He spoke of love, family, loyalty, communication and forgiveness.

We need to bring back the living room, he said. There needs to be a time in every home when families gather to be together, to hear each other, to see each other, to be in community. There needs to be a time when harmony rules and we fill a room with our collective light.

It used to take a guitar to do it, he said. Then a radio made the living room a gathering place. When television came along, we started to look at something other than each other. We began to separate, and it affected every neighbourhood, every community.

We need to bring back the living room. We need to make it a family room again. That's what Johnny Cash said to me that day, and I will never forget it. I will never forget him. That connectedness, that harmony, is how you change the world. My friend John told me that.

Butterfly Teachings

. . .

IT WAS THE BUTTERFLIES, my people say, who brought the first human babies to their feet. Before that, the New Ones sat in innocence beneath a tree, watching the world around them with wonder. But Creator had planned more for them. Their destiny called for them to move throughout the world. These human babies were meant to walk upon their two legs, and as long as they sat under that tree their destiny could not be fulfilled.

So the Animal People came.

The weasels came to dart and dance around the human babies. The babies just clapped their hands and laughed. Then the fox came, and in her wily way tried to cajole the babies into following her. But the human babies merely hooted in glee. The crows came, and they hopped and danced about in hopes that the New Ones would stand and join them. But the babies never moved.

Creature after creature arrived. Each one tried to entice the New Creations from their seat beneath that tree, and each one came up short. There was a seemingly endless parade of Animal People, and the human babies marvelled at all of them. But they wouldn't stand and walk.

Then, across the meadow, a brilliant cloud appeared. In the sunlight its colours danced and dipped and shone wildly. The New Ones watched this living rainbow approach, and they grew excited. The cloud seemed to float in all directions at once, and when it came near them the New Ones laughed like never before.

That cloud of butterflies drifted under the branches of the tree where the human babies were sitting. They fluttered among the leaves, dropping lower and lower until they were only inches from the New Ones' heads. They hovered there. The human babies reached out their arms to catch them. But the butterflies inched a little higher.

The air seemed to tremble with butterflies. The human babies were entranced. Each time they tried to snare a handful of colour, the cloud drifted away. They stretched their arms higher. They thrust out their hands. But it was to no avail. When the butterflies danced just out of reach a final time, the New Ones lurched to their feet and raced after them across the meadow.

The Animal People celebrated quietly, then returned to their dens and burrows and nests. The human babies never caught those butterflies, but they kept on running, right into the face of their destiny. Sometimes you can still hear them laughing in the sunshine.

I HEARD THAT STORY for the first time at a gathering of the Three Fires. In traditional times, the Three Fires was an alliance of the Ojibway, Odawa and Potawatomi nations. We met for a week's worth of activities geared towards perpetuating our traditional ways—what's called *Enendamowin,* or Ojibway worldview. For me, as a storyteller, it was a time to be guided in the principles and protocols of our oral tradition.

It was as if the butterflies were calling me forward to my destiny.

Sometimes you can get to thinking that the way you have come to know, the cultural, spiritual or philosophical way you accept as your own, is the only one with something to teach you. That was true for me for a while. I believed that there was value only in Indian things. It worked for a time. I found small glories in the expression of my native soul. I found people who were generous of spirit and I learned many things. But I had walled myself into a cultural wigwam, and as long as I sat there I couldn't run across the meadow. So the butterflies came again.

This time the butterflies came in the flow of notes from a keyboard. They sprang from the big hands of a black man who had never seen a wigwam. His name was Thelonious Monk, and I heard him play a song called "Epistrophy" on late-night radio. I was standing at my sink washing dishes when the cascade of notes rinsed all my thoughts away.

Monk played with his whole body. You could hear that. He played each note as though he were amazed at the one that preceded it. It was sensual, challenging music, and it required your full attention to follow it. Once you did, there was a world of musical shapes, textures and possibilities to reach for.

I became a jazz fan. I listened to jazz and I read about the music. I read about the people. When I started to read about the history of black music, I saw where the butterflies were leading me. I learned about field hollers, spirituals, the blues and the call and response choruses of a people chained.

Above all, I learned that soul is a universal experience. We discern that whenever we clamber to our feet and chase the butterflies.

To Love This Country

. . .

SOMETIMES YOU BREATHE this country in,
and the air of it is wild, free and open, like a ragged song.
I've heard that song in a thousand places.
In 1987, when I was a struggling freelance journalist.
I tracked down a famous artist then ensconced in the Jasper
Park Lodge and made arrangements to interview him.
Driving north from Calgary, through Banff and then on
through the glistening glory of the Columbia Icefield, I felt
the power of the landscape all around me.

Twenty miles south of Jasper I stopped to rest. I walked
through the woods towards the sound of waterfalls, and
what I found there was magnificent. I stepped out onto
a small table of stone above a chasm into which the water
tumbled. In the shaded light of mid-morning, I watched
the massive emerald and white and turquoise flume from
mere yards away. It was like levitating. What I heard in its
roar were spirit songs, the voices of my people in celebration of that pure fluid power. Later, in the living room of
his suite, I spent the afternoon and early evening with
Norval Morrisseau, talking about art and music and the
spiritual and traditional ways of the Ojibway.

I spent the winter of 1996 plowing through prairie snow along the cliffs above the North Saskatchewan River. I was teaching in Saskatoon, and I walked there to clear my head. The wind was raw and cutting, and it was through tears that I saw the bend of that river, felt its muscle from three hundred feet away. I heard its sibilant call to Hudson Bay, the echoed shouts of Indians and voyageurs riding on the crystal fog of ice.

I stayed with my friends Anne Doucette and Michael Finley that winter. She owned a bookstore and he taught at the university. Along with their son and daughter and Anne's mother, they welcomed me into their home. It was a sad time for me then, and walking eased the hurt. I'd plod through the winter chill, knee-deep in fresh prairie snow, and return to feel the warmth of welcome at their door. The light of their friendship was a song in itself.

In 1998, I spent five days in a canoe with an Inuk man named Enoch. We paddled a course of portages that the Algonquin people used to navigate their way through the territory north of Maniwaki, Quebec. There were a dozen of us in six canoes under the guidance of Algonquin guides and elders.

We paddled across a wide lake in a raging windstorm. Enoch and I battled mightily with waves higher than the gunwales of the canoe. Rain soaked us to the skin. In the shelter of a horseshoe bay, we drank black tea and felt the wind calm. That afternoon we shot a rapid, both of us energized by the challenge. We emerged into a long, flat cove where we fished and rested.

We camped that night on a mossy rock bluff surrounded by huge firs and pines. In the light of the fire I heard stories of an Inuk life. I heard music in the soughing of the wind through the trees, the soft slap of water at the foot of the bluff and the call of loons. The sheer loneliness that is the North and the comfort of a voice in the glow of firelight were grace notes all around us.

There is a song that is Canada. You can hear it in the bush and tree and rock, in the crash of a Pacific surf and the blowing of the breeze across a prairie sky. There are ancient notes in its chorus, voices sprung from Metis roots, Ojibway, Cree, Micmac and then French, German, Scottish and English. It's a magnificent cacophony.

I have learned that to love this country means to love its people. All of them. When we say "all my relations," it's meant in a teaching way, to rekindle community. We are part of the great, grand circle of humanity, and we need each other.

It wouldn't be Canada with one voice less.

Firekeeper

. . .

THERE'S AN OLD cast iron wood stove on the corner of the deck. It used to heat this cabin, but it's been replaced by a newer, more efficient model. So now it's a firepit we sit in front of on long, cool summer nights or in the more clement evenings of winter and fall.

To sit there in the hushed air of evening is to be transported. Fire is funny that way. It connects us to a primeval part of our being. Our conversation always slows, stops sometimes, as we stare into it, watching the flames flicker and dance. Somewhere in our genes lives the memory of a fire in the night. Somewhere in the jumble of our consciousness is the recollection, dimmed by time and circumstance, of a band of us huddled around a flame for security, warmth and community. We all share that. No matter who we are today, we began as tribal people. That's the truth that fire engenders.

I learned that in the mid-1990s. I was attending the annual spiritual gathering in Algonquin territory in Mani-waki. Our host was elder William Commanda, a globally recognized teacher, and we'd come from all corners, from all peoples, to share four days of ceremony, ritual and unity.

Each day featured an opportunity to sit with elders and spiritual teachers from a handful of First Nations. The time from sun-up to sundown was filled with guidance. The teachers showed us ancient spiritual ways, still alive and vital, and allowed us to participate in rituals that began in deep prehistory. Everywhere you could see acolytes sitting in humble silence at the knee of the carriers of knowledge. But the centrepiece of the gathering was the sweat lodge grounds.

Each teacher built a lodge and held ceremonies there throughout the day. With their apprentices, they made that ancient ritual available to as many people as possible. There were at least a dozen domed lodges, and the smell of smoke and sacred medicines, the sound of prayer and petitions to the Spirit World, was everywhere. It felt like holy ground.

A sweat lodge, in its simplest sense, is a sacred edifice. It's shaped like a womb, and when you strip yourself down and crawl into it on your hands and knees, you return yourself to the innocence in which you were born. You return yourself to genuine humility. The darkness you sit in is a symbol of your unknowing, and the rocks glowing in the pit represent eternal, elemental truth.

It's not a ceremony to be taken lightly. It's not a sauna. It's not some charming throwback. Instead, it's a gateway to the truths within you and a path to the spiritual truths that govern the universe. It's a place of prayer, of sacrifice, of enduring, of healing and if you're fortunate, of insight.

An elder I had worked with previously arrived late
one evening. He asked if I would be his helper, and I agreed.
When the sun came up we began to build his lodge. He was
patient and generous, taking his time in teaching me the
traditional protocols of building a sweat lodge. I was deeply
honoured. While we worked, he told me stories and talked
about how the ceremony had evolved for the northern
Ojibway.

When we were finished he asked me to be his firekeeper.

In the traditional way, acting as a firekeeper is an
honoured role. You build the fire that heats the rocks used
in the ceremony. Your prayers around that fire are the first
prayers in the process. You prepare the ritual. You take
care of everything so that the teacher can focus, and when
the time comes you watch over the participants. You stand
guard outside that lodge while the ceremony runs, attentive,
ready to serve, and you pray along with the petitioners
in the lodge.

Ernie liked a hot ceremony. His lodges asked the utmost
of participants, and the heat in them was tremendous.
Quite often people could not endure it and surrendered long
before the usual four rounds of prayer and song and talk.
They would crawl out of the lodge when I opened the door,
weak, spent and vulnerable. My job was to tend to them.

They were German, Finnish, English, French,,Ojibway,
Cree, Metis and Algonquin. But stretched out on the

ground, struggling for breath, crying, ashamed, perhaps, they were just people, human beings in need of care. I cradled heads and offered water. I applied cool cloths. I spoke softly and encouragingly. I helped people stand and walked them to shade.

I did that for four days, and at the end, when there was just Ernie and me, praying and singing in the lodge, I offered thanks for that incredible privilege.

Up until then I had been adamant that native things stay native things. I had fought so hard to reclaim the displaced parts of myself that I believed no one else had a right to the things that define and sustain us. Our spirituality was *our* spirituality. Being a firekeeper taught me different.

We are all travellers searching for the comfort of a fire in the night. We are all in need of a place of prayer, of solace, of unity. Our fire burns bright enough for everyone.

Ceremony

. . .

THERE IS a medicine bowl in our living room.
Tobacco, sage, sweetgrass and cedar are mixed together
in that bowl for prayer and blessings. With the touch of
a flame, smoke climbs and billows around us and, when I
close my eyes to pass it over my body, time folds in upon
itself, transports me to a time beyond time. Some days I
can't remember how I lived without it, this easy ceremony.

I went to a Salvation Army church when I was a small
kid. Sunday school seemed to fit me, and I was eager
to return every week. The stories were captivating, and I
loved to sing. We learned all the big-beat hymns like "Jesus
Loves Me," "This Little Light of Mine" and "Onward,
Christian Soldiers." Something in the music called to me,
and I responded.

When I was adopted, I was peeled away from that influence. I learned Presbyterian hymns after that, staid and
proper and stern. I felt lonely for the lilt of the Army tunes.
The Presbyterian canon meant strict regimentation in study,
work and daily life. There was no room for choral glee.

As a teenager living on the streets, I attended an evan-
gelical church for a short time. A program called Teen

Challenge took me in and introduced me to their doctrine, but their hand-clapping jubilation came along with talking in tongues and a severe discipleship. I lasted a few weeks, then ran back to my concrete world. A friend introduced me to the Jesus Freaks in the early 1970s. I liked their long hair and the remnants of the flower power mentality, but something in all the post-psychedelia made me sad. Scientology was big in the early '70s, too. Then came the teachings of Ram Dass and Krishnamurti and the poetry of Khalil Gibran. After that was the huge swell of life-affirming therapies. I practised Transactional Analysis, tried Gestalt therapy, read *Born to Win* and books by B.F Skinner, Carl Rogers, Rollo May and Leo Buscaglia. I read everything from *I'm OK, You're OK* to *Zen and the Art of Motorcycle Maintenance*. Everywhere I went someone was into something, and I veered sharply towards anything that promised an answer. Nothing seemed capable of filling me, though, giving me detail. I learned about a lot of intriguing processes, but I couldn't find the ease and comfort that I craved.

Then along came Albert Lightning. He was a Cree traditional teacher and elder who had been a political leader at one time. When I met him, he was leading a workshop at the Indian Ecumenical Conference in Morley, Alberta. I talked to him for a long time one night. I told him about my search, about the hollowness in my chest and in my life.

He taught me about ceremony that night. He took some tobacco, sweetgrass, sage and cedar, told me about their properties and how they were meant to be used. He told me about the principles they represented and about how living by those principles was the true Indian way. Through the ceremony of the medicine bowl, he taught me how to pray in gratitude, to ask for nothing, to be thankful instead for all that was present in my life right then and there. Then he told me to take the spirit of that small ceremony out into the world with me.

Anyone can be spiritual in a quiet room, but out in the world is where the challenge presents itself. If you can learn to take the humility, gratitude and silence you find in the medicine bowl ceremony into the world, you can live a principled life. When you live a principled life you learn to live spiritually. When you learn to live spiritually you find harmony with people. Then life itself becomes a ceremony. That, in the end, is what it's all about, this Indian way, this journey.

When we smudge ourselves on these mountain mornings, my woman and I, we join ourselves to the great wheel of energy that exists all around us. And I am filled.

The Sharing Circle

. . .

THERE'S A CIRCLE of stones in our front yard.
The dog and I gathered them one day in the old pickup and
brought them here from an area near a remote lake higher
up in the mountains. The stones are of various types and
textures, and they form the rim of a garden I planted for
my woman's pleasure.

Within the garden are plants, flowers and grasses
suited to the arid heat. As summer edges into fall, they're
tall and thick and colourful. The display draws humming-
birds, bees and butterflies. It's a magnificent circle of life,
and it took tending to get it this far.

My people say that all things form a circle. Life is a
circle that moves from the innocence of childhood and back
to it again, in the quiet wisdom of elderhood. The energy
we call Great Spirit moves in a great unseen circle around
us. That's why the bowl of a ceremonial pipe, a sweat lodge
and a Medicine Wheel are round. The circle, they say, is
the model of the universe.

In my late forties I lived in a condo in Burnaby, British
Columbia, amid the sharp angles of the metropolis. How
isolated the geometry of the modern world makes us

all. There's a rigidity to straight lines, and when you live within them long enough you can't help but be affected.

I spoke to the pastor of a downtown church about it. It was a United Church called the Longhouse Ministry that ministered to urban native people and others who were marginalized. I expressed my concern that we weren't speaking to each other any more. I told him about a simple ceremony I'd been instructed in a long time before.

It's called a Sharing Circle. It's open to everyone, a safe place to gather, to speak and be heard. It's a place of prayer and ritual guided by ancient spiritual protocols aimed at creating harmony. In the Sharing Circle we can share about our common human experience, its joys and sorrows, and offer the power of our words and emotions to each other. The pastor and I agreed that the community could benefit from something like that.

We put up posters and gave out pamphlets for a few weeks before the first gathering. I described the circle to organizations over the telephone. I e-mailed, faxed and visited in person. When the night of the first circle arrived, my woman and I were anxious. We didn't know what to expect.

It was a rainy night, cold, on the cusp of winter. We arrived a half hour early, and as I'd been instructed, I smudged the area with sacred medicines, said a prayer and centred myself on the push of positive energy. We wanted desperately to share the hope we felt, the strength we'd both found in the traditional teachings of my people and the vision of harmony we held for the planet.

When people began to arrive, we were amazed. They were a glorious conglomeration. There were urban native people, dispossessed of their cultures and traditions. Along with them came a university professor, a carpenter, a schoolteacher, a working single mother, a grandmother and a businessman. All of them gathered shyly in that circle, silent, maybe skeptical and afraid.

We sat in candlelight. When the ceremony started and a prayer was said, you could feel everyone relax. Taking up a hand drum, I explained the nature of the circle. I told them that the guiding principle was equality. We were all brothers and sisters, all looking for a linchpin, a way to focus our lives. Then I sang a prayer song.

What followed stays with me still. I explained how the ceremony was created to allow every voice the opportunity to be heard. The circle was a sacred space for every hurt, every joy to find expression, I said. It was a teaching way to show us how similar we are, how joined. Then I passed around an eagle-wing fan, and each person had a chance to share.

We heard stories of pain. We heard of struggle. We heard of confusion and doubt and unknowing. Some people spoke of gratitude, their relief at finding a place where unspoken things could be surrendered. As the talk continued the sounds of the city disappeared, even though we were half a block away from a major thoroughfare. We sat in a deep communal silence to listen to each other. When the ceremony ended with a final drum song, a prayer and hugs all around, not a single person wanted to leave.

We carried on that simple ceremony for the better part of three years. Every time it was the same. The energy of the people, their desire for talk, for connection, for harmony, created a magnificent spiritual sense we all carried away. We learned that no one of us is ever far away from others, that we all carry the same baggage in life, that when we allow ourselves to hear each other, we are joined forever.

Everyone has a story. That's what the circle teaches us. We become better people, a better species, when we take the time to hear them. That's how you change the world, really. One story, one voice at a time.

Stripping It Down

. . .

WHEN WE CAME to this cabin we had to leave
our old life behind. We had to disassemble everything,
strip away the clutter of life. A painting that had seemed
relevant in a city context became unnecessary here. Books
that had marked our footsteps on a cosmopolitan journey
lost their importance in the presence of bears. The transition surprised us both. We'd come to believe we needed all
that stuff to define us. But in the end it was just stuff. We
donated curios, mementoes and random objects to good
causes, gave them to friends or tossed them away. What we
were left with were the essentials.

Oh, there's the usual collection of things still. We have
a television and a stereo, and we've held onto the art that
retains its original frankness. We have a laptop and a PC,
and we get our Internet signals from a satellite. Our occa-
sional jaunts back to the city are made in a Subaru. But we
shop less now, and what we bring home is, for the most
part, only what we need. Food. Water. The stuff of life.

When I first began my journey to reclaim my culture,
I thought I needed a conglomeration of stuff to make me an
Indian. I thought I had to live my life with an Indian motif,
with native art, native books, native music and native
fashion all around me. So I collected roomfuls of stuff.

But when I started to attend ceremony and met traditional teachers, I confronted an astounding simplicity. Everything in my world was elaborate, shiny. But the teachers I found were nothing like that. Sometimes it was only the braids in their hair that bore any stamp of Indianness. I wondered about that. I wondered how you could be authentic without the signature. I wondered how you could be an Indian without the trappings, the visual statement of your being. So I asked.

A wise Ojibway man named Art Solomon told me to gather a yard of cotton cloth, some ribbon, a pair of scissors and a can of tobacco. I was to make this gathering my mission, the sole focus of one day. Then I was to find a quiet place where I felt secure. I was to go there with my gathered articles and sit.

I was to ask myself why my question was important, why I felt it necessary to move to knowledge. More importantly, I was to examine how it felt to not carry the answer. Once I'd discerned that, I was to cut a small square of cloth with the scissors, then take a pinch of the tobacco, place it in the cloth and tie it with ribbon.

This small tobacco tie would symbolize my question and my emotional and spiritual need. When I returned to Art I was to offer the tobacco. I could ask my question once the tobacco was accepted. It seemed odd, quaint, charming in a folksy kind of way. But I did it.

True learning requires sacrifice. That's what the tobacco offering taught me. That was the intent of the ritual. That's why Art asked me to make that offering. On my quest for understanding, I had to sacrifice my time and my money. I had to sacrifice my pride by confronting the truth of my unknowing. In the end I had to sacrifice my humility by reaching out for help in understanding.

That ceremony stripped away the stuff that blocked me from myself. I could see that it didn't matter how I looked or what I wore. What mattered was the nature of my question, and how I felt about it. I had to strip things down in order to hear the answer. When I did, I learned that what I needed was far less than I had, far less than what I desired, and it freed me.

I didn't become more Indian by learning that—only more human.

BOOK FOUR

ISHPIMING

(UNIVERSE)

EVERYTHING IS ENERGY. This is what our teachers say.
Great Spirit is the feeling of that energy expressed in all
things, radiating everywhere around us. To stand upon the
land is to feel joined to it, to become a part of that wheel
of creative, nurturing energy. In the Long Ago Time, Star
People brought us teachings. When they returned to their
home we were left to gaze across the universe and feel
the truth of what they had given us. Everything is energy.
We are all one being. We are all one soul, and we need each
other. That is spiritual. That is truth. That is Indian.

Neighbours

. . .

THE LAKE HERE has tempers and moods. When the wind is right, it can whip itself into white-caps. Other times, an easterly breeze will let the water be languid. A slight southwesterly push can create speckled channels. When it's placid, the lake hangs like a mirror between the poke of mountains.

It's a shape-shifter, this lake. Like all living beings, it breathes and moves and changes. It slides from azure to grey, indigo, cobalt, moss green or even silver, depending on the weather and the light. In storms it has a purple cast, and once last fall it took on a deep, melancholic blue, like yearning.

The lake is what draws people here. The community that's grown up around it is small, mostly former city dwellers like us, disgruntled with the speed and noise and smell of things urban. Our homes lean towards the rustic, and improvements happen gradually, as time and finances permit. Everyone is thrifty with their time.

There are the motorized outdoorsmen, too, the particular breed who can only appreciate nature at thirty miles an hour from an ATV, dirt bike, snowmobile or powerboat. But they mostly keep to themselves. If they chop down the odd beautiful tree or bulldoze a lovely copse of aspen to make room for their toys, we've learned to let it be.

My woman and I came here in the late summer of 2005. It took us a year or so to completely shrug off the city, but from the beginning our time here was marked by a downshift of energy. Despite ourselves, we would slip into idle, appreciating the symphony of land and silence. Now the place has rooted us.

We never learned about our neighbours in the city beyond simple elevator courtesy and chit-chat. Everyone was just too busy. Out here it's remarkably different.

Across the road are the Haggartys. John and Penny commuted to the city for a few years, but the long drive and the urban hustle and bustle grew to be too much. So they built a log home and settled in. With local jobs, they're fixtures now.

We met them soon after we arrived. John walks their two dogs down the road in the mornings, and he and I spoke right away. It wasn't long before we were sharing dinners, telling our stories and becoming friends. Getting to know them has been a pleasure. They're in their fifties, like us, seasoned by mortgages, career dips and dives, aging and other life lessons. They still tour on their motorcycle, ski some in the winter, love the land, love each other and hold out hope for long and agile senior years ahead.

Down the road a ways are Merv Williams and Ann Sevin. They have a pair of border collies named Tai and Chi and a twenty-foot lake barge. We met them at another neighbour's fiftieth birthday party. We were taken right away by their lack of facade, any need to be anything other than who they are. They are genuine. Staunch as old pines.

Merv has been a cowboy, a rancher and an outdoorsman all his life. At sixty-seven, his time on horseback is over now, and there's a note of sadness when he speaks of it. But he's always on the land, and he clearly loves it. He's a real raconteur, telling stories with zip and verve. Ann was a businesswoman. The border collies are named after her favourite activity. Arthritis in the knees has slowed her down some now. She can't ski, can barely climb stairs, but she remains vital and fun. When the four of us get together to float around the lake, fishing, talking, barbecuing, time takes on a different quality. We fall together easily, joined by the harmony of the natural world.

And there are other neighbours: Annie the weaver; Muriel and Pete, the local oldsters; and Rick and Anna Gilbert. He's an old-time fiddler and she's a Mississippi Cajun with an accent you can cut with a knife. All of them cherish the privacy the lake affords.

We're here, around this mountain lake, because the land has the uncommon ability to make everything make sense. We breathe easier here. We're here because life, when you listen to it, asks you to move a little slower, take a little more time, reach out a little more often to those around you.

We've learned to be neighbours here. We make eye contact. We wave. We share things. We help each other. We learn each other's stories and make them part of our own because, in the end, it's all one great, grand tale.

The Doe

. . .

THE LAND IS a sacred being. The land is healing, and she returns you to original form. She eases her
way into the cracks and crevices of you. She seeps into
the gaps that worldly understanding leaves, soothes the
raw spots, the urban rasp you've come somehow to accept
as natural. She reconnects you to the web of creation, as
familiar as a soft voice in the darkness.

That all came startlingly clear one recent morning.
It had rained the night before, and there was a palpable
freshness to things. Colours and shapes were sharpened by
the cut of the air and sound carried magnificently. The dog
and I set out for our morning walk, awed as always by the
ever-changing face of our surroundings.

A quarter mile down the gravel road is a sweeping
turn that's made tighter by the thickness of the bushes and
trees that push out to its borders. When we came around
the arc of it, a deer stepped out of the bush and stared at
us. I commanded the dog to sit, and she dropped to her
haunches immediately. The deer stood twenty feet from
us, ears swivelling and nostrils flaring for scent. None
of us moved beyond that.

She was a mule deer, a doe, and she had a satiny summer coat of tan with a thin ridge of black along the top of her neck. She was mature, with the confidence of several years behind her. As the dog sat staring at her, she raised her head slightly and continued to watch us in return. Satisfied that there was no danger, she moved closer.

The dog is a terrier, a hunter, a chaser, but she sat at the edge of the road quietly, enthralled by the appearance of this magnificent creature. She didn't bark, she didn't growl or whimper at the opportunity to run and chase and play. Instead, she sat with her head tilted, studying the deer. The deer looked at her, then at me, and edged closer again.

A timelessness descended on that moment. It took me back to moments from my boyhood when wandering the bush was like meditation. It was a return to the time when there were no barriers, when, as my people say, there were just the animals and all was harmony. Behind us we could hear the loons on the water, the nattering of squirrels in the trees and the crows and ravens in their garrulous conversations high in the branches. Everything was still. As I breathed, it was as if I could feel the air move between us.

In Ojibway the deer is called *Way-wash-ka-zhee*, the Gentle One, and its medicine power is nurturing. I said her name quietly in my language and eased my hand up towards her. She stepped closer. The dog maintained her silent sit. Slowly, the deer eased forward until she was eight feet away from us. I saw her sharply then, felt her curious, gentle power.

The sound of a truck on the gravel broke the spell.
The deer startled, but she looked back at us as she broke for
the depths of the bush. In that glance was a knowing,
a recognition of a peace encountered and carried forever.
There was no threat, no difference, only a crucial joining,
a shared breath of creation.

See, we don't become more by living with the land.
Instead, we become our proper size. It takes unity to do
that. It takes the recognition of the community we live in.
This world. This earth. This planet.

Rules for Radicals

. . .

WE LOVE TO SKI. Sun Peaks Resort is a short
drive from our cabin, and we head there as often as we can
in the winter months. As soon as we are on the chairlift
with our feet off the ground, we're exhilarated.
We enjoy the view as much as the action. It's spectacular from the top. You can see right across the Rockies, and
your imagination sends you soaring. The plummet down
the runs affords other panoramas.

Skiing is about freedom. It's about surrendering to
gravity and transcending it at the same time. It's the joy of
a headlong rush and the sublime ease of a traverse through
the trees in the crystal burst of brilliant, fresh powder.

So it was hard one day when the protesters came.
There's a land claim issue at the resort, and a band of
young native people, dressed in camouflage, arrived with
drums, pamphlets and megaphones. They stood at the base
of the mountain and harangued the families gathered to
enjoy the hill. In their masks, balaclavas and mirrored sun-
glasses, they were unapproachable and aloof. They looked
hugely ironic against that fresh, open landscape.

No one listened to them. No one paid any attention except the Mounties, there to make sure there were no confrontations. There weren't. The dozen or so protesters marched through the resort village, singing a drum song, waving flags and being ignored. Later, as we were taking off our gear in the parking lot, they marched past in a bedraggled line and disappeared into a small rusted bus.

It was a sad sight for me. I understood their cause. I understood their politics. I understood their motivation. I just didn't agree with the process.

In my early twenties I became a militant. I had discovered my people and reconnected with them. The people I met were angry. Native politics was in a boil. The American Indian Movement was making big headlines in the United States, and that energy had filtered into Canada. There were occupations, marches and other forms of protest.

As a displaced person, I was eager to fit in. I needed to be seen as native, so I adopted the politics. I pulled it around me like a cloak. I became red-minded. I grew my hair, dressed like I thought an Indian should and read the literature that the angry young people I met recommended: Vine Deloria's *God Is Red* and *Custer Died for Your Sins: An Indian Manifesto* and Dee Brown's *Bury My Heart at Wounded Knee*. After that I read Karl Marx, Eldridge Cleaver's *Soul on Ice*, Ralph Ellison's *Invisible Man* and *The Autobiography of Malcolm X*. I studied the writings of Abbie Hoffman and Bobby Seale to educate myself in the politics of struggle.

Back then I believed that once I had the rhetoric in place, the passion would follow. Everyone around me was angry, and I believed that to qualify as a native person I had to be angry too.

Then I came across Saul Alinsky's *Rules for Radicals*. His book contained less than what its title suggested, and at first I was disappointed. Then I read it over again, and I started to understand that radicalism isn't necessarily the mechanics of anger. Instead, it is the need of a people to invoke justice in the system through a certain generosity of spirit. It is, as Alinsky suggested, a process of communication.

I didn't know what that meant at first. Back then I was sold on the energy of the movement. The movement was all about bringing down the system, which was to blame for everything my people had suffered for hundreds of years. Change had to be brought about abruptly. My head was filled with the politics of retribution.

But Alinsky said something marvellous. He encouraged the younger generation to hang onto laughter, the most precious part of youth. Out of that, he said, we could find together what we were looking for—beauty, love and the chance to create.

His words resonated with me. I was angry because I thought I was supposed to be, because it was the Indian thing to do. By Alinsky's definition, that was method acting. Deep within me, where I truly lived, was a wish for peace. It took some doing, but through hard work and listening to the bona fide teachers in our native circles, I got in touch with that wish.

It's not necessary to bridge gaps between communities. Bridges rust and collapse. If, as a people, we work earnestly to fill those gaps with information, filling it in layer by layer with our truth, the gaps eventually cease to exist. Saul Alinsky taught me that. Life, like skiing, is about surrendering to gravity and transcending it at the same time.

Scars

. . .

THERE WAS A time, my people say, when the
animals prepared to abandon humans. A time before time,
when the role of animals as teachers was being ignored and
they decided to leave the Human Beings to their fate.

It wasn't an easy choice. The animals had come to love
their human brothers and sisters, their fanciful ways, their
dreams, their painful desire for learning. The humans were
like cubs and kits and hatchlings. The animals doted on
them and taught them to survive. But the Human Beings
outgrew that love and began to follow their own path.

This hurt the teachers greatly. They'd been instructed
by Creator to introduce the People to the world, and being
held in disregard caused them anguish. They knew the con-
sequences of such a course, and when they could not halt
the Human Beings on their path, the animals prepared to
leave.

But the dog told the Human Beings about the plan, and
they changed their ways. The animals returned to their
role as teachers, and the destiny of the People was changed
forever. Animals live around us still, and in their examples
lie the teaching ways of harmony, balance, sharing and
sacrifice.

I GOT A HAIRCUT the other day. For a few years now I've gone without the long hair and braids I wore for years. I've grown accustomed to shorter hair in my early fifties. It feels good, calming. The things my long hair represented exist within me now, and there's no need for outward symbols.

This time around I asked for a brush cut. As the barber shaved close to the sides and back, I enjoyed the feel of the razor. When it was over I held a hand mirror up to examine his work in the big mirror on the wall.

I could see the back of my head clearly. What I saw were scars, irregular white scars in four or five places. I knew they were there. I'd just forgotten about them, and seeing them so starkly was shocking in a way. I put my hand back there and ran my palm over them and remembered.

I got the first scar when I was seven. I'd been told not to climb the big birch tree that sat over a boulder near my foster home. But it was a challenge to all the kids in the neighbourhood to scratch our initials into the trunk. The kid whose initials were the highest was champion. I climbed that tree one day with a penknife in my teeth. I made it past the last set of initials and inched upwards another foot or so on the thin branches. But one branch broke, and I crashed down the length of that tree and cracked my head on the boulder. It cost me seven stitches and grounded me for a week or so.

I got the next scar when I was ten. I was playing pick-up hockey without a helmet, and a high cross-check ended in five stitches and a ban from playing for months. Back then the hottest stars in the National Hockey League went without helmets, and I wanted to mimic their speed, finesse and courage.

When I was nineteen I was helping a friend paint his house in St. Catharines. I climbed an extension ladder to paint the gable ends on the third floor. He'd told me to secure the ladder at the top, but I was in a hurry. A gust of wind caused me to lose my balance, and the ladder slid along the roofline. I crashed onto the veranda roof. That was worth five stitches and a good chewing-out from my very worried friend.

The other scars have a less elegant history. In a bar fight in Winnipeg in the late 1970s, a baseball bat to the back of the head cut me for nine stitches. Another time, drunk and staggering, I fell backwards onto the boulders along the river outside Calgary. That slip-up brought me six stitches and a slight concussion.

There are scars on different parts of my body, too. There's a long curved one above my left knee where a knife grazed me. That was in Thunder Bay in the 1980s. On my right knee is a leaf-shaped scar where I landed on a broken wine bottle in Toronto in 1974. Above my left eye, concealed by my eyebrow, is a scar from a police baton wielded during a protest in 1978.

There was a time, my people say, when the animals prepared to abandon humans. As a species, we've never been too great at listening. It's always taken a crisis to get our attention and return us to order and balance. I learned too often through injury. Sometimes the scars were visible, other times they were buried in my spirit. The second kind were slower and harder to heal.

I live more gracefully now. Around me in these mountains are animals that run and jump, crawl and fly, swim and dive. In their examples I see the way I choose now to live in the world.

My Left Arm

. . .

SOME MUSICIANS ARE like surgeons. They
wield their soulfulness like a scalpel, slicing through the
fat of life to reveal the glistening bone of truth. It's why we
return to them, that neat laying open to what lies beneath.
There's an economy to such honesty. Only the very
special ones have it. Miles Davis had that for me. When
his horn cut through the air I felt exposed, and the pure,
vibrato-less keening of his trumpet was a healing force.
That driving, unwavering note, triumphant and clear,
became something I sought to create in my living.

My life had been the opposite of triumphant for a
long time when I first heard Miles. My family lived in the
bush when I was born. They were seasonal gypsies, moving
about our traditional territory according to need and game.
All the generations after those of my great-grandparents
had been placed in residential schools. There, the process
of excising the Indian had robbed them of their souls, and
they returned hollowed out, incapable any more of relat-
ing to the land in a holistic way. They moved about it like
ghosts prowling a mourning ground. They struggled to
maintain the last vestige of a traditional Ojibway life as
they waited for the land to heal them.

It didn't. It couldn't.

Rather, they became embittered, angry and drunk. By the time I was born, our tribal life had mutated into something ugly, and we kids were neglected, often abandoned and abused. The great spiritual way of the Ojibway had been expunged by the nuns and priests, and in its place was terrible hurt vented on those closest to you.

When I was still a toddler, my left arm was shattered and torn from its socket, the shoulder joint broken. It was 1955. The doctors at the hospital in Kenora had little time for another Indian kid from the bush, and they attended to me in only the most cursory way. As a result my left arm hung backwards. The palm of my hand was turned outwards, and it atrophied and shrunk.

By the time I was five my arm was next to useless. When I was seven the Children's Aid Society finally stepped in. They sent me to the hospital in Thunder Bay, where doctors rebroke my shoulder joint, turned the arm around so it would hang properly and attached a tendon taken from my ring finger to my thumb. My thumb muscles had atrophied, and the tendon allowed my thumb to move normally.

It was advanced surgery for 1963. My left arm was suddenly mobile. I could flex my elbow and my fingers, and for the first time I could play like an ordinary kid. But the muscles were gone and would never grow back.

My left arm was a stick arm. As I grew it stayed the same, except for its length. I was ashamed and secretive and hid it as best I could. I refused to wear short-sleeved shirts. I kept my jacket on even in the hottest weather. In photographs I always tried to turn my right side to the camera.

For me, my left arm was the sign of my inadequacy. It revealed the indisputable truth of my inability to ever measure up, to be normal. To hide it was the only way I could feel secure, and that security was fleeting at best.

I never knew what had happened to my arm. It wasn't until I was in my forties that the truth came out. Up until then it was a mystery how my arm had been ruined, and I created elaborate falsehoods about the origins of my handicap. With each denial, the acceptance that nurtures healing receded further into the distance.

My left arm remained ugly to me until I learned to see it differently. It took a therapist to get me there. Together we penetrated the dense clouds of memory, working through the name-calling, insults and pitying looks. I learned to appreciate the things that I had learned to do despite the great wounding. I'd become a good athlete. I'd learned to play guitar. I'd learned to type. I'd ridden horses, canoed, fished, hunted, worked at heavy labour and performed the day-in, day-out acts of living.

We heal. Indian and non, we heal. But we must risk being vulnerable to get to the glistening bone of truth— that we are responsible for our own healing. No one else can get us there, and there isn't enough money anywhere to buy it for us.

After all these years, I think my left arm is beautiful. It's no longer a sign of my inadequacy. Rather, it's a sign of my enduring spirit, my ability to win out over adversity, to become all that I can be, to survive. It's the pure, triumphant note of my living.

Planting

. . .

WHEN I WAS FOURTEEN, I had chores to do.
My main job was to take care of the grounds around my
adopted home. I mowed the lawn twice a week, weeded
flower beds and edged them, watered plants and raked,
hoed and shovelled whenever that was ordered. There was
always something that needed doing, and it seemed to me
that the land was a problem to be solved.

Everything I did was scrutinized. When my edging
wasn't plumb and perfect, I had to do it over again. If tiny
heads of new weeds had pushed through between the
marigolds and the begonias, I was scolded as lazy and irre-
sponsible. The flower beds had to be raked smooth, the
clods of earth battered with a hoe until they lay like sand.
Otherwise I earned no right to play. I never took to that
job. I couldn't. The judgements rinsed all the joy away.

After I left that home I laboured at a handful of jobs
that called me to the land, but I never picked up a hoe or a
shovel or turned a bed of earth. I preferred cutting, sawing,
trundling and carting. That was all messy work by nature,
and there were no ghosts of perfection lurking around
the edges.

In every place I called home through the years the most I did was cut the lawn if one existed. There were sometimes houseplants, and I tended those, but there was nothing in the maintenance of small pots and planters to stir up the resentment I still carried from the lawns and flower beds of my youth.

Then we came here.

When we first saw this place, it didn't seem like much. Just a cabin in the trees overlooking a lake, a mountain humped up behind it like an overseer. It called to us, though, and we found a way to make it ours.

Both of us had spent a lifetime searching for home. Both of us had been orphaned by circumstance, fostered away to those who didn't understand the cleft that forms in your soul when you're swept away from love. We had each struggled mightily to heal that rift, and here we had a chance to settle and focus.

At first we did the easy things. We graduated to building a set of steps and some lattice work around the bottom of the deck. In our second summer we renovated the living room. We tore out the old carpeting and laid down flooring, then painted. The place became an extension of ourselves.

The soil in the garden had been left untended for years. There were twitches of grass and weeds and leftover bulbs that shot up leaves but never flowered. The soil was dusty and dry. In the hands it was hard and unpromising.

We weeded that soil last year, then turned a shovel in it for the first time. A spume of dust rose when the lump of earth landed. But as we added nutrients and raked and smoothed the soil with our hands, we could feel it come alive again. We bent to work, planting impatiens and begonias and ferns. When I plunged my fingers into the earth and felt the soft, cool richness of it, I felt richness in myself, too. We did up pots of geraniums. We planted juniper. When we were done we stood side by side, hand in hand, surveying our work with satisfaction.

This woman and I had taken to the land again. We were one with it. We were planted. We were home.

Wind Is the Carrier of Song

. . .

WIND IS THE carrier of song. There's a push from the west that sends cumulus banks over the top of the mountain, and in it is the plunge and roll of surf five hundred miles off. The wind in the reeds and grasses sings a higher register. It's the whistle of river valleys and the descant sweep of air across the delta.

Days when the wind blows from the north there's the keening pitch of the barren lands and the basso rumble of thunder in the peaks of a place where even the wind is lonely. Easterly flows bring the slicing soprano born in the unfinished aria of plain and prairie. The south is a contralto, warm, luxuriant, rising off distant beaches.

My people say the wind is Mother Earth brushing her hair. If you've ever seen the dance of branch and stalk and foliage, you'll know it's an apt image; the tresses of her, alive with motion, singing with spirit.

They also say the wind is eternal. Within it are borne the sighs and whispers of ancestors. Within it is the exhalation with which Creator blew life into the universe. To take the wind into us, to fill our lungs with it, is to hold time as a breath. Every living thing is joined in this way.

We breathe each other. When I feel the wind on my face now, at age fifty-three, I feel time and story and song.

In 1955, when I was born, status Indians were still not allowed to vote in Canada, even though we'd volunteered by the thousands to fight for the country in two world wars. We were exempt from conscription, but we went anyway. Our soldiers returned as decorated heroes to a country that did not recognize our people as full citizens.

In the legislation that regulated our lives, the *Indian Act*, it stated that a person was defined as anyone other than an Indian. We were not people. Our humanity was dismissed. We needed to get permission to do things that our non-native neighbours took for granted.

It used to be that we were not allowed to gather in public. We were not allowed to hire a lawyer, organize politically or leave the reserve without permission. The houses we lived in were not ours. They were owned by the government, as was the land they sat on. We were paid, dutifully, the five dollars annually that was ours by treaty. We were supposed to get ammunition, too, but that never happened.

Things changed after 1960. We finally gained the right to vote, the right to free assembly, permission to organize political groups. We were able to travel to and fro without restriction. We'd become citizens.

All of this happened without my knowledge. I was like most other Canadians, oblivious to the events shaping the lives of my native neighbours. My adopted family did not see the need for me to mingle with my own people or learn my history. Like everyone, I got only the accepted version of Canada.

In 1969 a future prime minister penned the White Paper on Indian policy. Jean Chretien wanted to scuttle anything that allowed us to identify ourselves as valid nations of people. He wanted to repeal the *Indian Act*, dismantle the bureaucracy that maintained it, abrogate the treaties, pat us on the head and send us out into the mainstream. It's called assimilation. He called it forward thinking.

I was thirteen, almost fourteen at the time, worried about girls, fitting in, girls, belonging, girls, wearing what was cool. No one told me what Chretien proposed. No one told me what it meant. No one told me how it might affect me. No one offered anything but a resolute marching on behind the flutter of the flag.

That White Paper changed everything. Instead of going away, my people became more present. We began showing up at universities and colleges in greater numbers. It wasn't long before we had doctors, lawyers, teachers, journalists and politicians. Our political organizations gained strength and vision. We became a force for change in our country.

By 1973 I was on the road, busy trying to survive. Life was about the search for security, meaning and definition. Like everyone else I concentrated on myself and my needs. Only when I reconnected with my native family did I open my eyes. What I saw was a people empowered. I saw a people dedicated to showing that self-government was not something to be granted, it was something we were born with. I saw pride and focus and healing. I saw how much history I'd missed. My people's and Canada's. The two were intertwined, and I undertook to unravel that history, to see each strand clearly. I understood how blind my self-centredness and self-concern had made me, how little I understood of the real story. In this, I was just like everyone else.

What I learned made me proud of native people, proud to be a part of the great, grand story that is my people's history with Canada. What I learned, in the end, made me proud to be Canadian. We've endured it all together, and we've become stronger because of it, even if we don't readily see that.

The wind is the carrier of song. When it blows across this mountain lake, it bears the essence of the land and its people. The essence of time past, time present, time future. It is our breath. Everyone's. *Ahow.*

All the Mornings of the World

. . .

THERE ARE MOMENTS here when the light
fills you. When the sun floods across the peak of the far
mountain and throws everything into a veil of red, you
can feel the light enter you, lift you, become you. On
storm mornings when grey is the desolate cloak of the
world, you can feel the light slip between your ribs,
roil there, become your breath.

For a long time there was a shade of grey, a specific
tone of light that rattled me. It resided at the edges of particular mornings, and I could feel it like a chill, spearing its
way inside me. I was always a little afraid of mornings, a
little skittish at dawn for that reason.

The feeling was never constant. That was the perplex-
ing thing. It happened only sometimes, surprising me
with its intensity. I thought for a time that I was crazy. I'd
heard of phengophobia, the fear of daylight, but that didn't
explain the woe that certain shade of light created in me.
It was a purple feeling, sad, heavy and lonely.

Through therapy, I got to the root of it.

The feeling goes back to a day in 1958, when I was two.
My family struggled with an awesome burden. They'd had
the Indian stripped out of them by the residential schools,

and they felt ignorant and powerless. They'd been reduced to spiritual beggary, kneeling at the feet of the nuns and priests to beseech direction and fulfillment. Direction came in the form of rigorous discipline, harsh punishment and instilled religious fear.

They were told their way of life was dead; the new world had no room for Indians, only for obedient servants of the white God. They were told that their beliefs were wrong, and that nothing in their worldview held any more. They were told that to live as savages was an abomination they needed to be cleansed of. They were washed in the blood of the Lamb, astringent, scouring and lethal.

In the bush where we lived, my family wrestled with demons. They drank to exorcise those demons, to mute the ache of whips and beatings and abuse.

One day in February of 1958, everything came to a head. There was a load of furs to be sold. We were camped across the bay from Minaki, a tiny railroad stop along the Winnipeg River, 150 miles north of Lake of the Woods. The adults left us kids at camp to head to town.

My sister Jane remembers that there was a good supply of firewood and food, so at first it was okay. But days passed. The firewood dwindled and the food was gone. I was crying from the cold and hunger. Still the adults didn't return. As the days stretched on, the elder two kids, Jane and Jack, got worried. It was deep winter in the North, and without firewood we would freeze to death.

So one morning they piled Charles and me on a toboggan, covered us with furs and blankets, and pulled us across the snow and ice. It took hours to cross that bay. It was a grey morning, cold and bleak. My sister says it was only the effort of pulling us that kept her and Jack alive. I lay on my back on the toboggan with only my face stuck out in the freeze. My brother pressed up against me for warmth.

When we reached Minaki, my sister and brother hauled us up to the railroad station. The wind was bitter. We found a corner away from the cut of it and huddled there together. By the time the Ontario Provincial Police found us, we were nearly frozen. They turned us over to the care of the Children's Aid Society.

The woe that was triggered by the pallid light of dawn was the despair of a toddler, abandoned in the bush. It was the cry of a child, helpless, hungry and afraid. It was the grief of a separation never understood, never explained and never resolved. When I touched it again, I wept.

My family has never acknowledged the truth, and they never will: they got drunk and forgot about us. Owning that hurts too much, and dealing with hurt was not something they were taught in those schools supposedly meant to save them.

Me? I wake up now to the glory of all the mornings of the world. The seamless blend of light and air lifts me up, healing me.

The Forest, Not the Trees

. . .

IN THE MOUNTAINS just before sunrise, the
world is an ashen place. Trees loom in the near distance
like phantom sentinels. There are bears about. The berry
bushes are bent and torn by their feeding. A few care-
less neighbours have had their garbage strewn about their
yards. It's a bear's world now—all shadow and quiet
and solitude.

In this vapid light things lose definition. Only the road
jutting through it gives the bush perspective. Otherwise,
it's thick and tangled, unvanquished.

I used to fear the bush. That's a hard thing to say
when you're Indian. But there was a time when the forest
at night or in the gloom of pre-dawn terrified me. Vague
terrors hunkered in the stillness. It took years to understand why.

When I was very young, our family home was mostly a
canvas army tent held up by spruce poles. Boughs lined the
floor. As a baby, I was swaddled in a cradleboard with moss
and cedar. My siblings watched over me when the adults
were away. My protectors were my older sister, Jane, and

my eldest brother, Jack. My brother Charles was only two years older than me, a toddler himself. Our grandmother was busy taking care of the camp or chasing after our older cousins. So we were a unit, the four of us kids.

It should have been idyllic. But it wasn't.

My family members were filled with bitterness from their residential school experiences, and that unhealed energy erupted often in drunkenness and violence. When we were adults, my sister told me how she used to carry me when the four of us went to hide in the bush at night, while the adults raged and drank and fought at the nearby fire. In the mornings we'd creep out of the bush and return to the camp to eat and drink.

My father was an outsider. He was an Ojibway from Pine Falls, Manitoba, and because he was perceived to be alien he was hated by my mother's family. They beat him up when he came around, chased him off. We four kids were tarred with the same brush. We were terrorized. My brother Jack fought back as best he could, but he was just a boy. Jane watched over Charles and me, sneaking us out of camp whenever it looked like things were about to boil over again. But she couldn't protect us all the time.

One day my aunt Elizabeth broke my left arm and shoulder by jumping on me as I swung in a moosehide harness between two trees. I wasn't yet a year old. When I was a little older, she took me out into the bush alone. Jane followed her secretly, and she watched in helpless horror as my aunt tied me down and whipped me with tree branches until I was raw.

My uncle Charlie tried to drown Charles and me. He took us by the throats and held our heads underwater, bringing us up gasping and crying before ducking us down again. He was holding us down hard when another Ojibway man who happened to be passing by knocked my uncle down and stopped him.

There were other horrors to be endured, but those two marked me for life. My left arm is still damaged, and I still can't swim with my head submersed.

Those experiences made me afraid of the bush. I was fine in the daytime, but when night fell and darkness reigned, my terrors returned. I was small again, helpless, beaten and afraid.

I'm almost fifty-three now, and I'm no longer afraid of the bush at night. Therapists and counsellors talked me through those terrors and the lingering trauma they caused. My family still suffers. They never talk about those days. They choose to live in the belief that sufficient time passing makes crimes irrelevant. But it doesn't.

I have post-traumatic stress disorder from the events of those days, and things still trigger me. I still wrestle with childlike reactions to perceived threats, sudden changes and the feel of unsafe territory. I still work to overcome those fears, to heal myself, to embrace the forgiveness that allows healing to happen.

See, I forgave my family a while back. I understand that they are not to blame for the institutional pain that was inflicted on them. They are not to blame for the effects of history.

In the light of each new day we are given justice in equal measure, to dispense at our will, and its root is forgiveness. In the light of each new day all things are in balance. Harmony comes when you can see the forest, not the trees.

Living Legends

. . .

TODAY THE DOG and I stopped to inspect the
heavily laden branches of a mountain ash tree. The red
berries were swollen and plump. The branches were bowed
under their weight, and we could see the bears would come
to feed very shortly. The splotches of red were magnificent
against the green.

The berries were not uniform in shape. Some were
stretched into funnels. Others were oblong, elliptical or
round as balls. Some were clumped together, while others
hung alone from the branches like commas, punctuation in
the story of that tree. Seeing them, I remembered the tale
of the mountain ash.

In the Long Ago Time a winter descended that was
like no other. The cold crept under the robes of the people
like fingers and held their wigwams in a fierce grip. The
snow piled higher than ever before. In the darkness, as
their fires ebbed, people could hear the frozen popping
of the trees and the eerie stillness that followed. Nothing
moved in that great petrified world.

Hunting became difficult. Everywhere creatures sought
deep shelter from the cold, and hunters returned from

their journeys ice-covered, shivering and empty-handed. The people had made do with their stores from the summer before, but there was worry in the camps as the cold seemed to settle upon the land. They needed fresh meat to supplement their dwindling supplies.

But soon it was impossible to walk for more than a few minutes without freezing. Everyone kept to their wigwams, praying for an end to the cold. The wind howled mightily through those long, terrible nights, and there was talk of Windigos and supernatural monsters eager to feast on the shrivelled corpses of the people.

Then, one day, the people emerged to a morning bright and calm. It was still horribly cold, but the arctic wind had ceased. All around them, though, lay the bodies of animals who'd frozen in the night. Rabbits, foxes, marten, skunks and birds. The people wept at this calamity, and they asked their Wise Ones what to do.

The teachers told them to take the bodies of the fallen animals to the tree that served them best. Back then, the people fashioned their bows and arrows from the wood of the mountain ash. Their survival depended on that tree. The elders told them to take a bead of blood from each of the animals and drop it on the branches of the mountain ash.

People prayed over that ritual. They beseeched Great Spirit for a teaching, for a way of knowing that would guide them. They made offerings of tobacco. They sang songs in honour of the deep cold. And the next day the cold abated. When the hunters went out to seek food, they saw that the blood of the animals had turned into bright red berries on the mountain ash. Birds and other creatures were feeding on them. From then on, whenever a hard winter was on the way, the mountain ash bore more berries than usual, and the people could prepare.

According to the old story, the plentiful berries on the ash tree the dog and I stopped beside meant that I'd have to lay in lots of firewood and make sure the cabin was prepared for a long chill. When the Storytelling Moons of winter come, we'll need full cupboards and a good supply of books and music, the other things we require for our survival. The mountain ash berries were telling us that.

Playing with Your Eyes Closed

. . .

THE STARS ARE FLUNG across the heavens tonight like seeds of light. As they wink and glimmer in their bed of darkness, I can feel that ancient light fall upon my face.

I had a philosopher friend once who told me the root of the word "universe." Universe, he said, was actually two words in the original Greek. The first part, *uni*, meant one, and the second part, *versa*, meant song. One song. Standing here with my face pressed upwards, I can feel the hymnal pulse of that.

My love for music has always sustained me. Over the years, in the soundtrack of my life, there have been cellos in moments sublime and pure, French horns and clarinets in times when life was joyous, blue notes in the lesser times, moody piano rolls in periods of reflection. There's a song for every memory.

I always wanted to play music, too. I wanted to recreate the fabulous sounds I heard in my head and felt in my hips and my soul. There was a kid named Brian Walsh in the eighth grade who played guitar and sang, and when he wowed everyone at the talent show, I knew that's what I wanted to do. But when I asked for a guitar I was laughed at, told I couldn't carry a tune in a pail and had no rhythm. It was ridiculous, they said, to even try.

But the desire remained. Guitar players became my focus. At live concerts I watched them closely. When I listened to records I sometimes sat in the dark and followed the guitar parts with my hands. I could see myself playing, imagine myself creating music and enjoying the freedom that it represented.

I finally got a guitar when I was in my late forties. Those first chords were hard. My fingers ached and my wrist got sore. I fumbled about a lot, but as soon as I strummed a clean E chord and heard the root note of the blues pressed out through my fingers, I was hooked.

I spent hours every day teaching myself to play. I read books, watched videos, joined Internet guitar groups and downloaded the songs I wanted to learn. I put my ear close to the speakers and listened intently, trying to unlock the secret to making music happen. I could feel the music in me, and more and more I reached for that feeling through my hands.

But that childhood judgement haunted me. I doubted my new ability, doubted the possibility of a tuneless, rhythmless me ever being able to play. I got into the habit of watching my fingers, hunching over the guitar as they moved through chord progressions and runs and scales. I figured that if I watched my hands closely enough, I could force them to make the right moves.

After about a year of this, I played for a friend. He
sat and listened, and when I was finished he nodded and
clapped me on the back for a good job. He was a guitar
player himself, so his praise was good medicine.

Then he told me to play the same thing with my
eyes closed. I was stunned by what followed. Even though
I'd played that song hundreds of times before, I fumbled
it badly. It was unrecognizable as the song I'd learned.

"You need to learn to play without watching your
hands," he told me. "You need to trust the music that's
in you. When you watch your hands, you're not making
music. You're only making sounds. Music needs to be
free to be music."

I became a better guitar player after that. Learning
to play without watching my hands lent my music a grace
it never had before. I'm no professional, but I can carry a
tune and the music happens naturally.

Life's like that, really. When you bend into it deliber-
ately, controlling every move you make, it's hard to find
the flow. You can learn the right moves, follow the pro-
gression accurately, but there's no spontaneous joy
in it, no glee.

There's a song in all of us. On nights when the stars
cajole you, it strains against your ribs and throat. The trick
is to trust it. Close your eyes, feel it there and let it out.

Universe. One song. Your music joined with the music
of everything.

What It Comes to Mean

. . .

THERE ARE MORNINGS here when the quiet fills you. You walk the line of lake, cautiously not wanting to break the spell of it. There's mist on the water, and it drifts up off the rock, enveloping you.

In this stillness you swear you can hear the sounds of drums on distant hills. You close your eyes, and in the push of breeze there's the wail and chant of singers. This fusty shoreline holds in its smell something ancient, eternal, vast. You need only breathe that smell into you to become it.

There's nothing in your experience to match this deliberate taking in. You who have fought so hard to find a place here, a definition beyond what the skin implies, have never encountered such frank acceptance of being. Against the push of land, the sweep of it, you fit easily, like another shoot of grass. There's the sense in you that *this* is what it means to be Indian.

They've called you many things in your time on this earth. You've been savage, red man, First Person, Aboriginal, native, indigenous, an original inhabitant. You've been labelled, tagged, defined, categorized, filed and absorbed;

analyzed, probed, studied, examined, inspected and researched. Never have they called you by your name.

When you were young, they called you Itchybum. On those long purple summer evenings, the game was Cowboys and Indians, except for them you were an Itchybum. An Itchybum was a joke, a cartoon in their minds, because that was all they knew. So you ran, hightailed it, really, through the backyards of your boyhood, pursued by miniature heroes intent on bagging you.

In the schools they sent you to, they called you "special needs." They called you slow, awkward and remedial because of the shyness born of displacement. In the home where they placed you, you were called "adopted." No one ever translated that for you. They never explained the intent of it, never let you know that it means, plainly, to be accepted. All you came to know was that it meant being reassembled, rearranged, shaped into an image your skin made impossible.

Once when a new cousin asked you at a gathering, "Did you used to be an Indian?" they laughed, and you didn't know what to say.

At school and in your neighbourhood you were a wagon burner, a squaw hopper, a bush bunny, a dirty teepee creeper and sometimes, because they didn't know what to make of you, a chink. You didn't know how to react. Shame made you keep those names to yourself, to feel the hurt like a bruise and say nothing.

On the streets you ran to they called you a lazy, shiftless, stupid, drunken, welfare bum. They expected failure of you and, when you tried to keep pace, to learn, express and grow, they called you uppity, confused and immature. You need to learn your place, they said, but they never offered to help you find it.

In the shops, foundries and camps where you went to work, they called you Jack pine nigger. In the fights and brawls that came of that, you learned scrapping was exactly what they expected. It anchored their treatment of you, made it valid. Again, you did not know what to say.

You learned that labels have weight. You learned to drink so that you wouldn't have to carry those labels or feel them stuck in you like arrows. And in your drunken stumble the shutters on their homes snapped closed, because you'd become exactly what they expected.

When you found your people you became Ojibway. You became Anishinabe. You became Sturgeon Clan. You became Wagamese again, and in that name was a recognition of being that felt like a balm on the rawness where they'd scraped the Indian away. Ojibway. It resonated in you. It was a label that held the promise of discovery, of homecoming, of reclamation and rejuvenation.

Oh, you struggled to understand its meaning. Applied to your life it was another burden, a tag you felt you had to earn. Everything you chose became Indian. Everything you allowed into your world was native. When the tag sometimes did not adhere, you did not know what to say.

You were created to be three things, the Wise Ones in your circles told you then. You were created to be a male, an Ojibway, a human being. That is the truth of you, Creator's gift to you, never to be taken away. One truth that carries within it many truths. Since then you've learned to look for those truths wherever they might be: in culture, philosophy, tradition, books, songs, stories, ceremony, ritual and spirituality.

Standing in the mist off the water, feeling the land inhabit you, you understand now that what it means, this word "Indian," is life. Life, with all its wrong turns, poor choices, mistakes, sins, sorrows, triumphs and small glories. Accepting that, wearing it loose as an old blanket, is what gives you grace, what grants you identity.

You fit here. You belong. No matter what they call you.

Walking the Territory

. . .

THESE ARE THE DAYS of summer's end.
Above the mountains clouds are a heavy grey, ominous
with snow that's a mere month away. There's a washed-out
feeling to the blue sky now, and the jays and other winter
birds have begun to peck about the yard. Even loon calls
in the thick purple night are urgent now. Autumn moons.
Time to fly.

The morning air bears a nip as the dog trots back from
her foray in the trees, heaving fogs of breath. Mist shrouds
the lake. The black water speaks of ice and the deep glacial
dark of winter. Geese flap down the cleft of lake, angling
south, and beavers fatten up on saplings near the shore.

These are the days of melancholy, the air chilled and
bruised. As you walk the territory of your living, you're
saddened some by the dimming of the light but thrilled at
the power of change everywhere around you.

In the autumn of 1986 I walked the northern territory
where I was born. My uncle had told me where our camps
used to be, and I rented a boat and motor and headed down
the Winnipeg River. It was an important trip for me. I'd

been reconnected with my native family for eight years by then, but I had no sense of my beginnings, and I wanted to see where it had all started. There was something in those territories I needed. Exactly what that was I didn't know. I only knew that I needed to walk there.

The summer boaters had all disappeared by that time. There was only me on the water. Powering down the length of the river, I was awed by the incredible combination of fullness and emptiness. The land had a haunting quality. Mysterious secrets lurked in the trees and rocks and bog.

The water was dark, with a bottomless feel. I sensed the presence of big muskies and sturgeons and pike no farther away than the length of an oar. The day was overcast, with some breaks in the cover when the sun poked through. It illuminated rapids and swells and eddies, so that the spume of them glistened like frost against the hard black of the river's muscle.

When I found the cove across the bay from Minaki, I nosed the boat into it. There was only the ripple of the water and the wind in the trees. Everything else was silent. I cut the engine and allowed the boat to drift in to the thin gravelled stretch of beach. The land seemed to slip by, and there was the sense of time bending in upon itself.

No one had been there for some time. That was obvious from the overgrowth on the narrow trail that wound up from the beach. The trailhead was barely discernible.

Everywhere there were windfall trees and exuberant bursts of bracken and bramble and moss and lichen. I had never experienced such stillness.

I didn't know where to look for the campsite, so I settled into a steady prowling. The ground was rocky and hard to navigate. But I managed to cover a lot of it. The deeper I walked into the bush, the more I got the feeling of time suspended. Only my footfalls on the rock and twigs sounded in that thick unmoving air.

I could feel the land around me. There were no edges to it, no limits, no borders. I stood in the middle of its relentless unfurling, alone, vulnerable, humbled by its magnitude.

I walked for hours. Now and then I'd stop somewhere, sit against a tree and look around. Sometimes I just stood in the forest and felt its quiet power, its pervasive upwards thrust. I never did locate the old campsite, but I found something much more valuable. As I stood in that chill autumnal light, seeing my breath float into the dimness, I found the essence of my Ojibway self.

In the shadow and break of the land, I could imagine my people living. I could sense the discipline they needed to survive out here. I could sense the fortitude, the strength of will, the grit and determination the land asked of them. And I could sense the deep spirituality that it engendered, feel it like an ember from those tribal fires glowing at my core.

I boated later to other spots my uncle had suggested. On each trip to the place my history began, I gleaned more from the land. I never found a physical clue of my beginnings, but the fundamental psychic connection I made has never left me.

I am and will always be Ojibway. Anishinabeg. It is the identity Creator graced me with. What I become in this world is framed forever by that definition, just as it is rooted in the land from which I sprang. As long as there is the land there will always be a home for me, a place my soul can wrap about itself.

When we speak of land claims and treaty rights, this is what we mean. This way of returning to a place where history is a feeling, a spiritual presence that empowers, enables and sustains us. A point of contact with Creator. A prayer and a realization. When you walk the territory of your being, the truth is everywhere around you.